DAYS

Spiritual Practice

ADRIAN COX B.SC.

BALBOA.PRESS
A DIVISION OF HAY HOUSE

Balboa Press books may be ordered through booksellers or by contacting:

Balboa Press
A Division of Hay House
1663 Liberty Drive
Bloomington, IN 47403
www.balboapress.co.uk
UK TFN: 0800 0148647 (Toll Free inside the UK)
UK Local: (02) 0369 56325 (+44 20 3695 6325 from outside the UK)

Print information available on the last page.

ISBN: 978-1-9822-8804-4 (sc)
ISBN: 978-1-9822-8803-7 (e)

Library of Congress Control Number: 2023923253

Balboa Press rev. date: 12/04/2023

Contents

Introduction to 49 Days Spiritual Practice

The practice of engaging in a spiritual journey spanning 49 days is a profound and transformative endeavor that transcends cultural and religious boundaries. Rooted in the belief that a period of 49 days holds unique significance, this spiritual practice provides individuals with an opportunity for deep reflection, personal growth, and a heightened sense of connection to the spiritual world.

Throughout history, diverse cultures and faiths have embraced the symbolism of 49 days as a period of transition, spiritual purification, and rebirth. Whether it is the Bardo journey in Tibetan Buddhism, the 49-day mourning period in certain Asian traditions, or other spiritual practices around the world, the essence of this 49-day journey is a testament to the enduring human quest for understanding the mysteries of life, death, and the afterlife.

In this exploration of the 49 Days Spiritual Practice, we will delve into its significance, the rituals associated with it, and the diverse ways in which it is practiced in different cultures. We will also consider the potential benefits of embarking on this journey, including personal growth, emotional healing, and a deeper connection to the spiritual realm.

The 49 Days Spiritual Practice invites individuals to embark on a transformative voyage, one that encompasses not only the mysteries of existence but also the timeless quest to connect with the divine. Whether you are following a specific religious tradition or seeking a spiritual journey uniquely your own, the practice of 49 days offers a path toward self-discovery, enlightenment, and a profound connection to the eternal mysteries of life and death.

The Awakening Within

Welcome, dear reader, to this transformative journey of self-discovery and spiritual awakening. Over the next 49 days, we will embark on a profound exploration of the depths of your being, guiding you toward a greater understanding of who you truly are and awakening the dormant potentials within you.

Today, we start at the very beginning, with the recognition that you are more than just your physical body. You are a unique and radiant soul, temporarily inhabiting this physical form on your journey through life. It is essential to realize that your true essence transcends the limitations of your body and the boundaries of time and space.

Take a moment to center yourself. Find a quiet place, free from distractions. Close your eyes, take a deep breath, and exhale slowly. With each breath, release any tension, worries, or thoughts that may be clouding your mind. Let go of the external world and turn your focus inward.

As you continue to breathe deeply and rhythmically, imagine a warm and comforting light at the core of your being. This light represents your true self, your soul. It is eternal, boundless, and filled with wisdom and love. Connect with this inner light and feel its presence within you. This is the source of your true power and authenticity.

Now, ask yourself these questions and reflect upon them:

1. Who am I beyond my name, my roles, and my achievements?
2. What are the deepest desires of my soul?
3. What brings me a profound sense of joy and fulfillment?

4. What limiting beliefs or fears have held me back from embracing my true self?

Write down your thoughts and insights in a journal. This journal will be your companion throughout this 49-day journey, a place to record your experiences, revelations, and intentions.

As you continue to explore your inner world, remember that this is just the beginning. You are embarking on a sacred quest to awaken the dormant aspects of your being, to shed the layers of conditioning, and to rediscover your true purpose and potential.

Each day of this journey will bring new insights, challenges, and opportunities for growth. Embrace them with an open heart and a curious mind. Let your inner light guide you, for it knows the way to your highest self.

With gratitude and anticipation, we set forth on this path of awakening, trusting that each step will bring us closer to the profound realization of our true nature. May your inner light shine brightly on this first day and throughout this transformative journey.

Tomorrow, we will delve deeper into the nature of the mind and its role in our awakening. Until then, carry the awareness of your inner light with you, for it is the compass that will lead you to the depths of your soul.

Blessings on your journey, dear seeker of truth.

The Power of Awareness

W elcome back to our journey of self-discovery and spiritual awakening. Yesterday, we began to explore the essence of your true self, your inner light. Today, we delve into the profound power of awareness and its role in unveiling the depths of your being.

Awareness is the key that unlocks the door to your inner world. It is the light that shines on the hidden corners of your mind and heart, revealing the truths that have been obscured by the noise of everyday life. By cultivating awareness, you gain the ability to see yourself more clearly and to navigate the challenges of life with greater wisdom and grace.

Begin your day with a moment of mindfulness. Find a peaceful place where you can sit or lie down comfortably. Close your eyes and take a few deep breaths, grounding yourself in the present moment. As you breathe, let go of any tension or distractions.

Now, turn your attention inward. Imagine a gentle, illuminating light at the center of your consciousness. This light represents your awareness. It is pure, unbiased, and non-judgmental. Let it shine on your thoughts, emotions, and sensations, just like the sun illuminates the landscape.

As you observe your inner world, notice any thoughts that arise. Without judgment, simply observe them as if they are passing clouds in the sky. Your thoughts are not you; they are a part of your experience but not your essence.

Next, bring your awareness to your emotions. What emotions are present within you today? Are they light and joyful, or heavy and burdensome? Allow yourself to feel them fully, without resistance. Emotions are like the weather; they come and go, but your awareness remains constant.

Finally, bring your attention to your body. How does it feel physically? Are there any areas of tension or discomfort? Gently scan your body from head to toe, and as you do, send your breath and awareness to any areas that need attention, allowing them to relax and release.

In your journal, reflect on your experience of this mindful practice. Did you notice any patterns in your thoughts or emotions? Did you discover any areas of tension in your body that you were previously unaware of? Remember that the goal is not to change anything but to observe and become more intimately acquainted with your inner landscape.

Throughout the day, practice moments of mindfulness whenever you can. Whether you are eating, walking, working, or resting, bring your awareness to the present moment. The more you practice, the more you will awaken to the richness of your inner world and the interconnectedness of all things.

Awareness is the first step on the path to self-discovery and awakening. Tomorrow, we will explore the concept of self-compassion and how it can deepen your understanding of yourself. Until then, may your awareness continue to illuminate the path to your true self.

Blessings on your journey of awakening.

Cultivating Self-Compassion

Welcome to the third day of our journey towards self-discovery and awakening. Over the past two days, we have explored the essence of your true self and the power of awareness. Today, we delve into the transformative practice of self-compassion.

Self-compassion is the art of treating yourself with the same kindness and understanding that you would offer to a dear friend facing challenges or setbacks. It is a vital aspect of awakening to your true nature, as it allows you to embrace all facets of yourself, even those you may perceive as flaws or weaknesses.

Begin your day by finding a comfortable and quiet space. Take a few deep breaths to center yourself in the present moment. As you breathe in, imagine inhaling compassion and understanding. As you exhale, release any self-judgment or criticism.

Now, reflect on the following:

1. Recall a recent situation where you were hard on yourself or experienced self-criticism. What triggered these feelings, and how did they affect you?
2. Imagine that a close friend had experienced the same situation. How would you respond to them? What words of comfort and encouragement would you offer?
3. Now, turn that same kindness and understanding toward yourself. Write down what you would say to yourself in the same situation.

In your journal, record your reflections and the compassionate words you would offer to yourself. This practice is a powerful way to bridge the gap between your inner critic and your inner nurturer, allowing you to treat yourself with the same love and care you extend to others.

Throughout the day, be mindful of your self-talk. Whenever you notice self-criticism or negative self-judgment creeping in, pause and replace those thoughts with the compassionate words you wrote down earlier. Treat yourself with the same gentleness and love that you would offer to a cherished friend.

Remember that self-compassion is not about indulgence or avoiding personal growth. It is about acknowledging your humanity and allowing yourself to learn and grow from your experiences with kindness rather than harshness.

As you continue to cultivate self-compassion, you will find that your relationship with yourself deepens, and the barriers to self-discovery begin to crumble. Tomorrow, we will explore the importance of letting go of the past and forgiving yourself for any perceived mistakes or regrets. Until then, may your heart be filled with self-compassion and understanding on this journey of awakening.

Blessings on your path to self-discovery and self-compassion.

DAY 4

The Gift of Forgiveness

Welcome back to our journey of self-discovery and spiritual awakening. On this fourth day, we delve into the profound practice of forgiveness and the freedom it offers on the path to discovering who you truly are.

Forgiveness is a gift you give to yourself. It is the act of releasing the burdens of the past, freeing your heart from the weight of resentment, and creating space for healing and growth. When you forgive, you open the door to greater self-awareness and a deeper connection with your true essence.

Find a quiet and peaceful space to begin your practice of forgiveness. Close your eyes, take a few deep breaths, and allow yourself to relax. Visualize the person or situation that you feel the need to forgive. It could be someone else or even yourself.

As you bring this person or situation to mind, acknowledge the feelings that arise within you. Allow yourself to feel any anger, hurt, or resentment without judgment. These emotions are valid, and it's essential to honor them.

Now, imagine a warm, healing light surrounding both you and the person or situation you are forgiving. Visualize this light gradually dissolving the negative emotions and releasing the grip they have on your heart.

Repeat the following affirmations silently or aloud:

"I forgive you, [name or situation], not because your actions were justified, but because I deserve peace."

"I release the pain and resentment I have been carrying, allowing space for healing and growth."

"I choose to free myself from the chains of the past, embracing the present moment with an open heart."

As you recite these affirmations, feel the weight of resentment lifting from your heart. Imagine it dissipating into the light, leaving you with a sense of relief and freedom.

In your journal, write down your reflections on the forgiveness practice. How did it feel to release these negative emotions? What insights did you gain about yourself and your capacity for forgiveness?

Throughout the day, continue to practice forgiveness. If other situations or people come to mind, apply the same forgiveness process. Remember that forgiveness is not condoning or forgetting; it is a conscious choice to release the grip of the past on your present.

As you embrace forgiveness as a regular practice, you will find that your heart becomes lighter, and your inner world becomes more open to the truths of who you are. Tomorrow, we will explore the concept of self-love and its role in our journey of self-discovery. Until then, may forgiveness be a guiding light on your path to awakening.

Blessings on your path to self-discovery and forgiveness.

The Power of Self-Love

Welcome to the fifth day of our transformative journey toward self-discovery and awakening. Today, we explore the profound concept of self-love, an essential ingredient in unlocking the fullness of your being.

Self-love is not a selfish or narcissistic trait; it is the foundation upon which your spiritual journey is built. It is the practice of treating yourself with the same unconditional love and kindness that you would extend to a beloved friend or family member. When you truly love and accept yourself, you open the door to profound self-discovery and growth.

Begin your day by finding a quiet and peaceful space. Close your eyes, take a few deep breaths, and center yourself in the present moment. As you breathe, let go of any tension or distractions.

Now, bring your attention to your heart center, the place where love and compassion reside. Imagine a warm, radiant light at the core of your being, representing your self-love. Feel this light expanding with each breath, filling every corner of your being with love and acceptance.

Reflect on the following questions:

1. How do you currently treat yourself? Are you your own best friend or harshest critic?
2. What thoughts and beliefs about yourself hinder your ability to love and accept yourself fully?
3. What actions can you take today to practice self-love and self-care?

In your journal, record your reflections and your commitment to practicing self-love. Self-love begins with awareness and intention. It's a daily choice to treat yourself with kindness, gentleness, and compassion.

Throughout the day, be mindful of your self-talk and actions. Whenever you notice self-criticism or self-judgment creeping in, pause and replace those thoughts with loving and affirming statements. Treat yourself with the same tenderness you would offer to a dear friend.

Remember that self-love is not about perfection but about acknowledging your worthiness and embracing your imperfections as part of your unique journey. It is about nurturing your physical, emotional, and spiritual well-being.

As you cultivate self-love, you will find that your relationship with yourself deepens, and your capacity for self-discovery expands. Tomorrow, we will explore the importance of gratitude and its role in awakening to the richness of life. Until then, may your heart be filled with the warmth of self-love on this journey of awakening.

Blessings on your path to self-discovery and self-love.

DAY 6

Embracing Gratitude

Welcome to the sixth day of our transformative journey toward self-discovery and awakening. Today, we explore the profound practice of gratitude and its ability to open your heart and expand your awareness.

Gratitude is a powerful force that can shift your perspective from what you lack to what you have. It is the practice of acknowledging and appreciating the abundance that surrounds you, no matter how small or seemingly insignificant. When you cultivate gratitude, you create a positive and receptive space within yourself, allowing you to more fully experience the richness of life.

Begin your day by finding a quiet and peaceful space. Close your eyes, take a few deep breaths, and center yourself in the present moment. As you breathe, let go of any tension or distractions.

Now, bring your attention to your heart center, the place where love and gratitude reside. Imagine a warm, glowing light at the core of your being, representing your gratitude. Feel this light expanding with each breath, filling you with a sense of appreciation and joy.

Reflect on the following questions:

1. What are you grateful for in your life right now? Consider the people, experiences, and even the small everyday blessings.
2. How does expressing gratitude make you feel? How does it shift your perspective?
3. Are there any challenges or difficulties you've faced that you can find gratitude for? What lessons have they brought into your life?

In your journal, record your reflections and list at least three things you are grateful for today. It can be as simple as the warmth of the sun on your skin, the laughter of a loved one, or the air you breathe. The act of recognizing and expressing gratitude is a practice that deepens your connection with life itself.

Throughout the day, practice gratitude by noticing and appreciating the beauty and abundance around you. Take moments to express your thanks, either silently or aloud, for the blessings that flow into your life.

Remember that gratitude is not about denying challenges or difficulties but about acknowledging the goodness that coexists with them. It is a practice that can lead you to a deeper understanding of yourself and the world around you.

As you continue to embrace gratitude, you will find that your heart opens, and your awareness expands. Tomorrow, we will explore the importance of connecting with nature and the wisdom it holds for our journey of awakening. Until then, may your heart be filled with the richness of gratitude on this path of self-discovery.

Blessings on your path to self-discovery and gratitude.

Communion with Nature

Welcome to the seventh day of our transformative journey toward self-discovery and awakening. Today, we explore the profound connection between your inner world and the natural world that surrounds you.

Nature is a powerful teacher and healer. When you immerse yourself in the beauty and wisdom of the natural world, you can awaken to a deeper understanding of who you are and your place within the vast tapestry of life.

Begin your day by stepping outside and finding a quiet spot in nature, whether it's a park, a garden, a forest, or even your own backyard. Take a moment to breathe in the fresh air, feel the earth beneath your feet, and connect with the natural world around you.

As you immerse yourself in nature, pay close attention to the sights, sounds, and sensations that surround you. Notice the gentle rustling of leaves, the colors of the flowers, and the songs of the birds. Allow yourself to be fully present in this moment of communion with nature.

Reflect on the following questions:

1. How does being in nature make you feel? What emotions and sensations arise when you connect with the natural world?
2. Consider the intricate balance and harmony present in nature. How might this reflect the interconnectedness of all life, including your own?
3. In what ways can you bring more of the wisdom and tranquility of nature into your daily life?

In your journal, record your reflections and any insights gained from your time in nature. You might also jot down a few ways you plan to integrate nature into your daily routine, whether it's through walks, meditation, or simply pausing to appreciate the world outside your window.

Throughout the day, take moments to connect with nature, even if you can't spend extended periods outdoors. Find a houseplant to care for, watch the sunset, or listen to the sound of rain. Nature is always present, offering its gifts of beauty and serenity.

Remember that as you connect with nature, you are connecting with a part of yourself that is deeply rooted in the natural world. Just as the seasons change and the cycles of life continue, so too do the cycles of your own growth and transformation.

As we continue this journey of awakening, tomorrow, we will explore the importance of silence and inner stillness as a means of accessing deeper aspects of your true self. Until then, may your connection with nature nourish your spirit and guide you on your path of self-discovery.

Blessings on your path to self-discovery and communion with the natural world.

The Story of Samuel

Once upon a time, in a quaint little cottage nestled on the outskirts of a serene forest, lived a writer named Samuel. Samuel was not just an ordinary writer; he was a man deeply passionate about the art of storytelling. His connection to words ran deeper than ink on paper; it was a metaphysical bond that had grown over the years.

Every day, Samuel would sit at his wooden desk, overlooking the whispering trees and babbling brook outside his window. He would allow his imagination to soar, penning tales that transported readers to realms beyond the boundaries of ordinary reality. His words were like spells, weaving intricate tapestries of wonder and enchantment.

As the years passed, something remarkable began to happen. Samuel's relationship with writing evolved into something extraordinary. It was as though his devotion to storytelling breathed life into a metaphysical being. This being, named Morpheus, was a shimmering, ethereal figure, born from the very essence of Samuel's creativity.

Morpheus, with an otherworldly presence, would often materialize at the foot of Samuel's desk as he wrote. This being was an embodiment of profound metaphysical wisdom, speaking in riddles and parables that transcended human understanding.

One misty morning, as Samuel was wrestling with the opening lines of his latest story, Morpheus appeared. He was a luminous, ever-shifting figure that seemed to exist beyond the constraints of time and space.

"Samuel," Morpheus intoned in a voice like the rustling leaves, "The words you weave hold the power to shape not only your stories but the very fabric of existence itself. Within your tales, the boundaries of reality blur, and worlds are born anew."

Samuel stared in awe at Morpheus. "But what purpose does this serve?" he asked, his pen poised over the paper.

Morpheus smiled, a shimmering cascade of light and color. "It serves the purpose of enlightenment, my dear writer. Your stories are keys to unlocking the mysteries of the cosmos, teaching those who read them to see the world through the lens of wonder and possibility."

Over the years, Morpheus continued to appear, offering Samuel guidance and insight that surpassed the boundaries of human comprehension. Together, they explored the metaphysical depths of storytelling, delving into the very heart of creativity and its connection to the universe.

Samuel's stories grew in depth and complexity, touching the hearts and minds of countless readers. His words became a source of inspiration and transformation, guiding others on journeys of self-discovery and enlightenment.

And so, in that tranquil cottage by the forest, Samuel and Morpheus, the metaphysical being born of his love for writing, continued their extraordinary partnership. They crafted stories that not only entertained but illuminated the profound mysteries of existence, forever reminding humanity of the boundless magic that resides within the pages of a well-told tale.

DAY 8

The Power of Silence and Stillness

Welcome to the eighth day of our transformative journey toward self-discovery and awakening. Today, we explore the profound practice of silence and inner stillness as gateways to unlocking deeper aspects of your true self.

In the hustle and bustle of daily life, silence and stillness can be rare and precious gifts we give ourselves. They provide a sacred space for you to listen to the whispers of your soul, to find clarity in the midst of chaos, and to connect with the deeper layers of your being.

Begin your day by finding a quiet and serene place where you can sit or lie down comfortably. Close your eyes, take a few deep breaths, and let go of any tension or distractions. As you inhale, imagine yourself breathing in peace and serenity. As you exhale, release any worries or restlessness.

Now, turn your attention inward. Imagine a calm, expansive pool of stillness within your heart and mind. Picture this pool growing larger with each breath, spreading tranquility throughout your entire being.

In this state of inner stillness, allow your thoughts to settle like sediment in a pond, creating a clear, reflective surface. As thoughts arise, simply observe them without judgment, and then let them gently float away.

Reflect on the following questions:

1. What thoughts and emotions surface when you are in a state of silence and stillness? How do they inform your understanding of yourself?

2. Consider the importance of space and emptiness in allowing new insights and inspirations to arise. How can you create more mental and emotional space in your daily life?
3. What practices or activities can you incorporate into your routine to cultivate inner stillness and silence?

In your journal, record your reflections and any insights gained during your practice of silence and stillness. Also, note any ideas or inspirations that emerge during these moments of introspection.

Throughout the day, make an effort to incorporate moments of silence and stillness into your routine. You can do this through short meditation sessions, mindful pauses, or even by simply taking a few moments to appreciate the beauty of silence in your surroundings.

Remember that silence is not the absence of noise but the presence of inner peace. In this peaceful space, you have the opportunity to hear the whispers of your soul, to discover deeper truths about yourself, and to awaken to the wisdom that resides within.

As we continue this journey of awakening, tomorrow, we will explore the concept of intuition and how it can guide you on your path of self-discovery. Until then, may your moments of silence and stillness bring you clarity and connection with your true self.

Blessings on your path to self-discovery and inner peace.

The Inner Guide of Intuition

Welcome to the ninth day of our transformative journey toward self-discovery and awakening. Today, we explore the profound concept of intuition and its role as an inner guide on your path to discovering your true self.

Intuition is your inner wisdom, a subtle and powerful force that resides within you. It is the voice of your soul, offering guidance, insight, and clarity amidst life's complexities. Learning to trust and listen to your intuition is a pivotal step in awakening to the depths of your being.

Begin your day by finding a quiet and contemplative space. Close your eyes, take a few deep breaths, and center yourself in the present moment. As you breathe in, imagine inhaling clarity and guidance. As you exhale, release any doubts or distractions.

Now, turn your attention inward and focus on your heart center, the place where intuition often speaks most clearly. Picture a soft, radiant light there, representing your intuitive wisdom. Feel this light growing brighter with each breath, filling you with a sense of inner knowing.

Reflect on the following questions:

1. Think about a time when you followed your intuition and it led you in a positive direction. What was the outcome, and how did it feel to trust your inner guidance?
2. Consider a situation where you ignored your intuition and later regretted it. What lessons can you draw from that experience?
3. What practices or rituals can you incorporate into your daily life to cultivate a deeper connection with your intuition?

In your journal, record your reflections and any insights gained from contemplating your intuition. Also, jot down any intuitive nudges or hunches that arise during this exercise. Trusting your intuition is like strengthening a muscle; it becomes more reliable with practice.

Throughout the day, listen for the whispers of your intuition. When faced with decisions or uncertainties, pause and ask yourself, "What does my intuition tell me?" Pay attention to any subtle feelings, sensations, or inner voices that guide you.

Remember that intuition often speaks in whispers, so it requires stillness and attention to hear it clearly. Trust yourself and trust your inner guidance. Your intuition is your compass on this journey of self-discovery.

As we continue this journey of awakening, tomorrow, we will explore the power of dreams and the messages they may hold for your spiritual growth. Until then, may your intuition be a source of wisdom and insight on your path to self-discovery.

Blessings on your path to self-discovery and intuitive wisdom.

The Wisdom of Dreams

Welcome to the tenth day of our transformative journey toward self-discovery and awakening. Today, we explore the enigmatic world of dreams and their potential to offer guidance and insights into the depths of your true self.

Dreams are like messages from your inner self, speaking in symbols, metaphors, and emotions. They provide a unique window into your subconscious mind, revealing hidden fears, desires, and untapped potentials. Learning to decipher the wisdom of your dreams can be a profound tool on your path to self-discovery.

Begin your day by acknowledging the significance of your dreams. Before you go to sleep tonight, set the intention to remember your dreams and receive guidance from them. You may wish to keep a dream journal beside your bed to record your experiences upon waking.

Before going to sleep, find a quiet moment to reflect on the following questions:

1. What recurring themes or symbols have appeared in your dreams throughout your life? Are there any patterns that stand out to you?
2. Can you recall a dream that felt particularly vivid or significant? What emotions or messages did it convey?
3. How do you usually feel upon waking from a dream? Are there recurring emotions or sensations?

As you drift off to sleep, invite your dreams to reveal insights into your true self, your desires, and your unresolved questions.

Trust that your subconscious mind will work with you to provide the guidance you seek.

Upon waking in the morning, take a moment to record any dreams or fragments of dreams that you remember. Don't worry if they seem disjointed or nonsensical; often, the deeper meaning becomes clear through reflection.

In your journal, write down your dreams and any insights or emotions they evoke. Over time, you may start to notice recurring symbols or themes that can shed light on aspects of yourself you may not be fully aware of.

Throughout the day, continue to reflect on your dreams and any messages they may hold for you. Consider how these dream symbols and emotions might relate to your waking life and your journey of self-discovery.

Remember that your dreams are a bridge to your subconscious mind, a realm where your true self often speaks in a language of symbols and metaphors. As we continue this journey of awakening, tomorrow, we will explore the importance of creativity and self-expression as means of uncovering deeper layers of your authentic self. Until then, may your dreams be a source of insight and revelation on your path to self-discovery.

Blessings on your path to self-discovery and dream wisdom.

Awakening through Creativity and Self-Expression

Welcome to the eleventh day of our transformative journey toward self-discovery and awakening. Today, we explore the powerful role of creativity and self-expression in unlocking deeper layers of your authentic self.

Creativity is the unique spark within you, a force that allows you to express your innermost thoughts, feelings, and desires in a multitude of ways. When you engage in creative activities, you tap into a wellspring of authenticity that can lead you toward profound self-discovery.

Begin your day by acknowledging the importance of creativity in your life. Take a moment to reflect on the creative activities that bring you joy and allow you to express yourself. Whether it's painting, writing, singing, dancing, or any other form of artistic expression, creativity is a gateway to your inner world.

Today, set aside some time for a creative endeavor that resonates with you. It could be a few moments of spontaneous doodling, writing a poem, or even cooking a meal with love and intention. Whatever form of expression you choose, allow yourself to fully engage in the process.

As you immerse yourself in this creative activity, reflect on the following questions:

1. How does creativity make you feel? What emotions or sensations arise when you engage in creative expression?
2. What ideas or inspirations arise during your creative process? Do they offer insights into your true self or your current life path?

3.   How can you incorporate more creativity and self-expression into your daily routine?

In your journal, record your reflections and any insights gained from your creative experience. Consider making a commitment to regular creative practices that allow you to connect with your authentic self on a deeper level.

Throughout the day, remember that creativity is not limited to traditional art forms. You can infuse creativity into all aspects of your life, whether it's the way you dress, the way you communicate, or the way you approach problem-solving.

Creativity is a powerful tool for self-discovery because it encourages you to explore the uncharted territory within yourself, to take risks, and to embrace vulnerability. It allows you to access hidden aspects of your true self that may be waiting to be revealed.

As we continue this journey of awakening, tomorrow, we will explore the importance of self-care and nurturing your physical, emotional, and spiritual well-being. Until then, may your creative expressions guide you toward a deeper understanding of your authentic self.

Blessings on your path to self-discovery and creative self-expression.

Nurturing the Self through Self-Care

Welcome to the twelfth day of our transformative journey toward self-discovery and awakening. Today, we explore the profound practice of self-care and how it nurtures your physical, emotional, and spiritual well-being, facilitating the awakening of your true self.

Self-care is an act of love and compassion directed toward yourself. It involves taking deliberate steps to care for your physical health, nourish your emotional needs, and tend to your spiritual growth. When you prioritize self-care, you create a harmonious environment for your true self to flourish.

Begin your day by acknowledging the importance of self-care in your life. Reflect on the areas of your well-being that require attention and nurturing. It could be your body, mind, emotions, or spirit.

Today, set aside some time for self-care activities that resonate with you. This might involve activities like exercise, meditation, a soothing bath, journaling, or simply spending quality time in nature. Whatever form of self-care you choose, ensure that it replenishes and rejuvenates you.

As you engage in your chosen self-care activities, reflect on the following questions:

1. How does self-care make you feel? What emotions or sensations arise when you prioritize your well-being?
2. Are there any self-care practices that you have neglected or wish to incorporate into your routine?
3. How can self-care become a regular and sustainable part of your life?

In your journal, record your reflections and your commitment to practicing self-care regularly. Consider creating a self-care plan that outlines specific actions you can take to nurture your physical, emotional, and spiritual health.

Throughout the day, be mindful of the importance of self-care. When you care for yourself, you are better equipped to face life's challenges with grace and resilience. It is not a selfish act, but rather a way to ensure that you are operating from a place of wholeness.

Remember that self-care is an essential aspect of self-discovery. As you nurture your physical body, calm your emotions, and deepen your spiritual connection, you create a fertile ground for the awakening of your true self.

As we continue this journey of awakening, tomorrow, we will explore the significance of relationships and how they mirror aspects of ourselves that are seeking recognition and healing. Until then, may your self-care practices be a source of strength and nourishment on your path to self-discovery.

Blessings on your path to self-discovery and self-care.

DAY 13

Reflections in Relationships

Welcome to the thirteenth day of our transformative journey toward self-discovery and awakening. Today, we explore the significance of relationships and how they serve as mirrors reflecting aspects of ourselves that are seeking recognition and healing.

Relationships are like a canvas upon which we project our inner world. They provide us with valuable insights into our beliefs, patterns, and emotions, offering us the opportunity to grow, evolve, and awaken to the truth of who we are.

Begin your day by acknowledging the importance of relationships in your life. Consider the various relationships you have—with family, friends, colleagues, and romantic partners—and their roles in your personal growth.

Today, take some time to reflect on your most significant relationships. Think about the following questions:

1. What do your relationships reveal about your beliefs, fears, and desires? How do they reflect aspects of your inner world?
2. Are there any recurring patterns or challenges in your relationships that you've noticed? What might these patterns be trying to teach you about yourself?
3. How can you approach your relationships with greater awareness and a willingness to learn and grow?

In your journal, record your reflections and insights about your relationships. Consider how you can use these insights to foster healthier, more meaningful connections with others and to deepen your understanding of yourself.

Throughout the day, be mindful of your interactions with

others. Pay attention to any emotional reactions or triggers that arise in your relationships. Instead of reacting impulsively, take a moment to reflect on what these reactions might be revealing about your inner world.

Remember that relationships are a powerful catalyst for self-discovery and personal growth. When you approach them with an open heart and a willingness to learn, you can unlock the potential for profound transformation and healing.

As we continue this journey of awakening, tomorrow, we will explore the concept of forgiveness in the context of relationships and how it can liberate you from the chains of the past. Until then, may your reflections in relationships guide you toward a deeper understanding of your true self.

Blessings on your path to self-discovery and awareness in relationships.

Liberating the Heart
Through Forgiveness

Welcome to the fourteenth day of our transformative journey toward self-discovery and awakening. Today, we explore the profound practice of forgiveness within the context of relationships and how it can liberate your heart and soul.

Forgiveness is a powerful tool for personal growth and healing. When you hold onto grudges, resentments, or past hurts, you carry the weight of the past into your present and future. By choosing to forgive, you release these burdens and create space for love, compassion, and understanding to flourish.

Begin your day by acknowledging the significance of forgiveness in your life. Reflect on the relationships or situations where forgiveness may be needed, whether it's forgiving others or forgiving yourself.

Today, dedicate some time to the practice of forgiveness. Find a quiet and peaceful space, close your eyes, and take a few deep breaths to center yourself in the present moment.

As you breathe, bring to mind a person or situation that you feel the need to forgive. Visualize this person or situation before you, and imagine a warm, healing light surrounding both you and them.

Repeat the following affirmations silently or aloud:

"I forgive you, [name or situation], not because your actions were justified, but because I deserve peace."

"I release the pain and resentment I have been carrying, allowing space for healing and growth."

"I choose to free myself from the chains of the past, embracing the present moment with an open heart."

As you recite these affirmations, visualize any negative emotions or burdens associated with the person or situation dissolving into the light, leaving you with a sense of relief and freedom.

In your journal, record your experience with the forgiveness practice. Reflect on any emotions or insights that arose during this process and how it felt to release the weight of past grievances.

Throughout the day, continue to practice forgiveness whenever it is needed. Forgiveness is not about condoning or forgetting, but about releasing the grip of the past on your present and future. It is a profound act of self-love and liberation.

Remember that forgiveness is a gift you give to yourself. By forgiving, you create space for love, compassion, and healing to flow freely, both within yourself and in your relationships with others.

As we continue this journey of awakening, tomorrow, we will explore the importance of embracing change and the growth that can come from surrendering to life's natural flow. Until then, may forgiveness be a guiding light on your path to self-discovery.

Blessings on your path to self-discovery and the liberation of the heart through forgiveness.

The Story of Emma

Once upon a time, in a place that existed where nothing was something, there was a peculiar town named Nullington. In Nullington, the residents embraced the concept of nothingness like no one else in the world. They lived their lives in a paradoxical manner, cherishing the emptiness and void that surrounded them.

The town itself was an enigma, composed of transparent structures that seemed to dissolve into the ether. Roads and pathways led to nowhere, and signs bore inscriptions that meant absolutely nothing. Yet, the townspeople found meaning in this nothingness. They would gather in the town square, sit in empty chairs, and converse about the absence of topics. They took great pride in their talent for discussing nothing as if it were the most profound subject in the universe.

One sunny day in Nullington, the townsfolk held their annual "Nothing Festival." The main event featured a contest to see who could do the most nothing. People would sit perfectly still, not moving an inch, their minds devoid of thoughts. The winner, of course, was the one who achieved the highest level of nothingness.

As the day wore on, the competition intensified. Contestants sat in various postures, some adopting the lotus position, while others simply slouched in their seats. The judges, with their blank expressions, watched closely. Hours passed, and the air grew still, as if the entire town had become one with the nothingness.

Finally, a young woman named Emma emerged as the victor. She had entered a state of perfect nothingness, so profound that even her fellow townspeople could barely perceive her existence. Her prize was a trophy made of transparent glass, a symbol of her mastery over nothing.

As the festival ended, the people of Nullington returned to their daily lives, content with their unique existence in a world that thrived on something. They knew that embracing nothing allowed them to appreciate the something even more. And so, in their town of paradoxical emptiness, the residents continued to celebrate the art of doing nothing, finding meaning in the absence of it all.

DAY 15

Embracing Change and Surrender

Welcome to the fifteenth day of our transformative journey toward self-discovery and awakening. Today, we explore the importance of embracing change and the growth that can come from surrendering to life's natural flow.

Change is an inevitable part of life. It brings both challenges and opportunities, and how we navigate change often determines our capacity for personal growth and self-discovery. Surrendering to the ebb and flow of life allows us to release resistance and open ourselves to new possibilities.

Begin your day by acknowledging the inevitability of change in your life. Reflect on past experiences of change and how they have shaped you into the person you are today.

Today, embrace the practice of surrender. Find a quiet and peaceful space, close your eyes, and take a few deep breaths to center yourself in the present moment. As you breathe, let go of any resistance or attachment to specific outcomes.

Visualize yourself standing at the edge of a flowing river, representing the ever-changing nature of life. Observe the water as it flows effortlessly, adapting to obstacles and curves in its path. Imagine yourself stepping into the river, surrendering to its current.

Reflect on the following questions:

1. What areas of your life do you resist change the most? Why do you think this resistance exists?
2. Can you recall a time when embracing change led to personal growth or a positive transformation? What lessons did you learn from that experience?

3. How can you practice surrender in your daily life, allowing life's natural flow to guide you toward self-discovery and growth?

In your journal, record your reflections and your commitment to practicing surrender. Surrender does not mean giving up; it means relinquishing control and trusting that the universe has a plan for you.

Throughout the day, remind yourself of the river's flow and the practice of surrender. When faced with changes or challenges, take a moment to breathe deeply and let go of resistance. Embrace the idea that change can be a powerful catalyst for self-discovery and personal growth.

Remember that by surrendering to life's natural flow, you open yourself to new opportunities and deeper levels of understanding about who you are and your purpose in this ever-changing world.

As we continue this journey of awakening, tomorrow, we will explore the importance of self-reflection and the role it plays in uncovering your true self. Until then, may surrender be your guiding principle on your path to self-discovery.

Blessings on your path to self-discovery and surrendering to life's flow.

Self-Reflection and Inner Wisdom

Welcome to the sixteenth day of our transformative journey toward self-discovery and awakening. Today, we explore the importance of self-reflection as a means of uncovering your true self and tapping into your inner wisdom.

Self-reflection is the art of turning your gaze inward, examining your thoughts, emotions, and experiences with the intention of gaining insight and understanding. It is a powerful practice that allows you to connect with your inner world and access the wisdom that resides within you.

Begin your day by finding a quiet and contemplative space. Close your eyes, take a few deep breaths, and center yourself in the present moment. As you breathe in, imagine inhaling clarity and wisdom. As you exhale, release any mental clutter or distractions.

Now, turn your attention inward, like a lantern shining light into the depths of your consciousness. Reflect on your thoughts, emotions, and experiences. Allow them to arise without judgment.

Consider the following questions:

1. What thoughts have been occupying your mind lately? Are there recurring themes or patterns in your thinking?
2. Reflect on your emotional landscape. How have you been feeling, and what might be contributing to those emotions?
3. Are there any recent experiences or events that have had a significant impact on your life? What lessons or insights can you draw from them?

In your journal, record your reflections and any insights gained from your self-reflection. Regularly practicing self-reflection can help you become more attuned to your inner world and the guidance it offers.

Throughout the day, continue to cultivate self-reflection. Take moments to pause and check in with yourself. Ask yourself how you are feeling, what you are thinking, and what your inner wisdom may be trying to communicate.

Remember that self-reflection is a practice that deepens over time. It allows you to navigate life's challenges with greater clarity and resilience. By tapping into your inner wisdom, you can make more aligned choices on your path of self-discovery.

As we continue this journey of awakening, tomorrow, we will explore the importance of cultivating patience and presence as we unfold the layers of our true selves. Until then, may self-reflection be your guiding light on your path to self-discovery.

Blessings on your path to self-discovery and inner wisdom through self-reflection.

DAY 17

Cultivating Patience and Presence

W elcome to the seventeenth day of our transformative journey toward self-discovery and awakening. Today, we explore the importance of cultivating patience and presence as we navigate the path of uncovering our true selves.

In a world filled with constant activity and distractions, patience and presence are rare gifts we can give ourselves. They allow us to fully experience the richness of each moment, to embrace the journey of self-discovery without rushing or resisting.

Begin your day by acknowledging the significance of patience and presence in your life. Reflect on how often you find yourself rushing through tasks, distracted by thoughts of the future, or dwelling on the past.

Today, commit to cultivating patience and presence in your daily life. Find moments throughout your day to pause, breathe, and be fully present in the moment.

As you engage in this practice, consider the following questions:

1. How does rushing through life or being preoccupied with the past or future affect your sense of well-being and your ability to discover your true self?
2. What activities or practices help you cultivate patience and presence? Are there specific times of day or places where you find it easier to be fully present?
3. How can you bring the qualities of patience and presence into your interactions with others, as well as into your relationship with yourself?

In your journal, record your reflections and your commitment to practicing patience and presence. Consider creating a list of activities or mindfulness techniques that help you stay grounded in the present moment.

Throughout the day, remind yourself to be patient and present. Whether you are eating a meal, engaging in a conversation, or simply walking in nature, make an effort to fully immerse yourself in the experience.

Remember that patience is not about waiting for something to happen; it's about embracing the journey and being open to what each moment has to offer. Presence is not just about being physically present; it's about being fully engaged and aware in mind, body, and spirit.

As we continue this journey of awakening, tomorrow, we will explore the importance of simplicity and letting go of unnecessary complexity as we seek to uncover our true selves. Until then, may patience and presence be your guiding companions on your path to self-discovery.

Blessings on your path to self-discovery and the cultivation of patience and presence.

DAY 18

Embracing Simplicity and Letting Go

W elcome to the eighteenth day of our transformative journey toward self-discovery and awakening. Today, we explore the importance of embracing simplicity and letting go of unnecessary complexity as we seek to uncover our true selves.

Simplicity is a gateway to clarity and self-discovery. In a world filled with distractions and demands, simplifying your life allows you to focus on what truly matters and create space for your authentic self to emerge.

Begin your day by acknowledging the significance of simplicity in your life. Reflect on the areas where you may have accumulated unnecessary complexity, whether in your daily routines, possessions, or relationships.

Today, commit to embracing simplicity in your life. Start by identifying one aspect of your life where you can simplify, whether it's decluttering your physical space, streamlining your daily tasks, or simplifying your relationships by focusing on what truly matters.

As you engage in this practice, consider the following questions:

1. How does simplifying your life create space for self-discovery and a deeper understanding of your true self?
2. Reflect on the benefits of decluttering your physical environment. How does it affect your mental and emotional well-being?
3. Are there any attachments or habits that no longer serve you and could be released to create more simplicity in your life?

In your journal, record your reflections and your commitment to embracing simplicity. Begin with small steps, and as you experience the benefits of simplicity, you may find yourself naturally letting go of more unnecessary complexity.

Throughout the day, be mindful of your commitment to simplicity. Notice how it affects your sense of calm and clarity. Embrace the feeling of lightness and freedom that comes with letting go of what no longer serves you.

Remember that simplicity is not about depriving yourself but about intentionally choosing what adds value and meaning to your life. By simplifying, you create a fertile ground for self-discovery and a deeper connection with your true self.

As we continue this journey of awakening, tomorrow, we will explore the significance of mindfulness and how it can lead you to a deeper awareness of your authentic self. Until then, may simplicity and letting go guide you on your path to self-discovery.

Blessings on your path to self-discovery and the beauty of simplicity.

DAY 19

Cultivating Mindfulness for Self-Discovery

Welcome to the nineteenth day of our transformative journey toward self-discovery and awakening. Today, we delve into the practice of mindfulness and its profound ability to lead you to a deeper awareness of your authentic self.

Mindfulness is the art of being fully present in the moment, paying attention to your thoughts, emotions, and sensations without judgment. It is a practice that fosters self-awareness and helps you connect with your true self by grounding you in the richness of each moment.

Begin your day by acknowledging the significance of mindfulness in your life. Reflect on how often your mind may be preoccupied with thoughts of the past or future, rather than fully engaged in the present moment.

Today, commit to cultivating mindfulness in your daily life. Find moments throughout your day to pause, take a few deep breaths, and be fully present in whatever you are doing.

As you engage in this practice, consider the following questions:

1. How does being mindful of the present moment help you connect with your authentic self? What insights have you gained from moments of mindfulness?
2. Reflect on the impact of mindfulness on your emotional well-being. How does it influence your ability to respond to situations rather than react?

3. Are there any areas of your life where you struggle to be mindful? What can you do to bring mindfulness into those moments?

In your journal, record your reflections and your commitment to cultivating mindfulness. Consider setting aside specific times each day for mindfulness practices, such as meditation, mindful breathing, or even mindful eating.

Throughout the day, remind yourself to be mindful. Whether you are engaged in a conversation, walking in nature, or simply savoring a meal, make an effort to fully immerse yourself in the experience. Pay attention to the sensations, thoughts, and emotions that arise without judgment.

Remember that mindfulness is a practice that deepens over time. It allows you to become more attuned to your inner world, your desires, and your authentic self. By grounding yourself in the present moment, you can navigate life's complexities with greater clarity and authenticity.

As we continue this journey of awakening, tomorrow, we will explore the significance of compassion, both for others and for yourself, as a powerful means of connecting with your true self. Until then, may mindfulness be your guiding light on your path to self-discovery.

Blessings on your path to self-discovery and the practice of mindfulness.

Cultivating Compassion for Self and Others

Welcome to the twentieth day of our transformative journey toward self-discovery and awakening. Today, we explore the profound practice of cultivating compassion, both for others and, importantly, for yourself, as a means of connecting with your true self.

Compassion is the gentle force that allows us to open our hearts to the suffering and joys of others. It is also a practice that, when extended to ourselves, can facilitate a deep and transformative connection with our authentic selves.

Begin your day by acknowledging the significance of compassion in your life. Reflect on moments when you have felt the warmth of compassion from others and its impact on your well-being.

Today, commit to cultivating compassion in your daily life. Find moments throughout your day to extend kindness and understanding to others, whether through acts of service, a listening ear, or a simple smile. Equally, remember to show yourself the same compassion.

As you engage in this practice, consider the following questions:

1. How does compassion, both for others and for yourself, foster a deeper connection with your authentic self?
2. Reflect on the times when you've been hard on yourself. How might self-compassion have changed those experiences?
3. Are there any areas of your life where you struggle to be compassionate, either toward others or yourself? What can you do to cultivate compassion in those moments?

In your journal, record your reflections and your commitment to cultivating compassion. Practice self-compassion by acknowledging and soothing your inner critic whenever it arises.

Throughout the day, remind yourself to be compassionate. In moments of frustration, stress, or self-doubt, extend the same kindness and understanding to yourself that you would offer to a dear friend.

Remember that compassion is a practice that deepens with time and effort. It allows you to connect with your true self by releasing judgment and embracing acceptance. By fostering compassion, you create a loving and nurturing space for your authentic self to flourish.

As we continue this journey of awakening, tomorrow, we will explore the importance of gratitude and how it can further illuminate the path to self-discovery. Until then, may compassion be your guiding light on your path to self-discovery.

Blessings on your path to self-discovery and the cultivation of compassion.

The Gratitude that Illuminates

W elcome to the twenty-first day of our transformative journey toward self-discovery and awakening. Today, we explore the profound practice of gratitude and how it can illuminate your path to self-discovery.

Gratitude is a radiant force that opens your heart to the abundance and beauty that surrounds you. It is a practice that allows you to see the blessings in every moment, fostering a deep connection with your true self.

Begin your day by acknowledging the significance of gratitude in your life. Reflect on the times when you've felt genuine gratitude and how it has affected your perspective and well-being.

Today, commit to cultivating gratitude in your daily life. Find moments throughout your day to pause and express gratitude for the people, experiences, and blessings in your life. Equally important, express gratitude for yourself and the journey of self-discovery you are on.

As you engage in this practice, consider the following questions:

1. How does gratitude foster a deeper connection with your authentic self by shifting your perspective from lack to abundance?
2. Reflect on a specific time when gratitude transformed your outlook or brought a sense of fulfillment. What were the circumstances, and how did it feel?
3. Are there any moments in your life, whether big or small, that you have yet to express gratitude for? How might acknowledging these moments enrich your self-discovery journey?

In your journal, record your reflections and your commitment to cultivating gratitude. Create a gratitude journal to capture the things you are thankful for each day, whether it's the beauty of nature, the kindness of others, or the inner strength you discover within yourself.

Throughout the day, remind yourself to be grateful. Pause and take a moment to express gratitude for the people who cross your path, the challenges that have shaped you, and the beauty that surrounds you.

Remember that gratitude is a practice that deepens over time, allowing you to connect with your true self by opening your heart to the abundance of life. It is a powerful beacon that guides you on your journey of self-discovery.

As we continue this journey of awakening, tomorrow, we will explore the significance of self-love and how it is essential for nurturing your authentic self. Until then, may gratitude be your guiding light on your path to self-discovery.

Blessings on your path to self-discovery and the illumination of gratitude.

The Story of Alex

Once upon a time, in a quiet, dimly lit room, Alex sat alone with a curious idea swirling in their mind. They had read about the concept of parallel timelines and wondered if it was possible to communicate with versions of themselves in different timelines to achieve a higher state of consciousness.

With a deep breath and an unwavering determination, Alex began their experiment. They dimmed the lights further, closed their eyes, and started meditating. As they delved deeper into their own consciousness, they visualized a vast network of timelines branching out before them.

In this meditative state, Alex could perceive glimpses of themselves in various timelines. Each version of them was engaged in different activities, making diverse choices, and leading distinct lives. It was like watching a web of infinite possibilities.

Alex reached out with their mind, seeking to connect with one of these versions. Gradually, they felt a connection forming, as if a bridge of thought linked them to a parallel self.

"Hello," Alex whispered into the void of their own mind.

A soft, distant voice replied, "Hello."

This voice belonged to a version of Alex who had chosen a path of spiritual exploration and meditation. They had achieved a higher level of consciousness, and their wisdom radiated through their words.

"What can I learn from you?" Alex asked, eager to absorb this newfound wisdom.

The other Alex began to share their insights about the nature of reality, the interconnectedness of all things, and the power of self-awareness. Each word was a revelation, and it resonated deep within Alex's core.

Over time, Alex continued to connect with different versions of themselves, each at varying levels of consciousness. Some were mired in negativity and self-doubt, while others had achieved incredible states of enlightenment.

As these conversations across timelines continued, Alex started to notice a transformation within themselves. They became more mindful, compassionate, and aware of the choices they made in their own timeline. The insights gained from their other selves provided a roadmap to a higher state of consciousness.

One day, while meditating, Alex felt a profound shift. It was as if all the wisdom, experiences, and lessons from their conversations had merged into a singular, transcendent understanding. They realized that the key to reaching a higher state of consciousness was not in escaping to another timeline but in embracing the present moment fully.

With this newfound clarity, Alex began to meditate with greater dedication, focusing on the here and now. Slowly, their consciousness expanded, and they experienced a sense of oneness with the universe. It was a state of enlightenment they had sought all along.

In this higher state of consciousness, Alex understood that the answers they had sought were always within themselves. By connecting with their own past and potential selves, they had unlocked the door to a deeper understanding of existence. They had become a beacon of wisdom, guiding others on their own journeys toward enlightenment.

And so, in the quiet of that dimly lit room, Alex's journey through the timelines had led them full circle, back to the present moment where they had awakened into a higher state of consciousness. The conversations with their other selves had served as stepping stones on their path to self-realization, reminding them that the most profound discoveries were often found within.

The Essential Practice of Self-Love

Welcome to the twenty-second day of our transformative journey toward self-discovery and awakening. Today, we delve into the essential practice of self-love and how it plays a crucial role in nurturing your authentic self.

Self-love is the foundation upon which self-discovery and personal growth are built. It is the act of embracing yourself, flaws and all, with compassion, kindness, and a deep appreciation for your uniqueness. By cultivating self-love, you create a fertile ground for your true self to flourish.

Begin your day by acknowledging the significance of self-love in your life. Reflect on the times when you've felt truly loving and accepting toward yourself, as well as the moments when self-criticism and doubt took over.

Today, commit to cultivating self-love in your daily life. Find moments throughout your day to be kind and gentle with yourself, as you would with a dear friend.

As you engage in this practice, consider the following questions:

1. How does self-love nurture a deeper connection with your authentic self by fostering acceptance and kindness toward all aspects of your being?
2. Reflect on a time when practicing self-love helped you overcome a challenge or transform a negative self-perception. How did it feel to be your own ally in that moment?
3. Are there any areas of your life where self-love is lacking? What can you do to infuse those areas with greater self-compassion and self-acceptance?

In your journal, record your reflections and your commitment to cultivating self-love. Create a self-love journal to capture moments of self-appreciation and self-acceptance, no matter how small they may seem.

Throughout the day, remind yourself to practice self-love. When faced with moments of self-doubt or self-criticism, pause and offer yourself words of kindness and understanding. Treat yourself with the same love and respect you would offer to someone you deeply care about.

Remember that self-love is not selfish; it is an act of self-care and self-preservation. By nurturing your own well-being and self-worth, you empower yourself to authentically engage with the world and continue your journey of self-discovery.

As we continue this journey of awakening, tomorrow, we will explore the importance of stillness and the quiet spaces within us as we seek to uncover our true selves. Until then, may self-love be your guiding light on your path to self-discovery.

Blessings on your path to self-discovery and the essential practice of self-love.

DAY 23

The Gift of Stillness and Inner Sanctuary

Welcome to the twenty-third day of our transformative journey toward self-discovery and awakening. Today, we explore the profound gift of stillness and the quiet spaces within us as we seek to uncover our true selves.

In the midst of life's busyness and noise, stillness offers us a sanctuary—a place to retreat, reflect, and connect with our innermost being. It is in these moments of quiet that we often find the deepest insights about ourselves.

Begin your day by acknowledging the significance of stillness and the role it plays in your life. Reflect on the times when you've sought solace in moments of silence, and the sense of calm and clarity it brought.

Today, commit to cultivating stillness in your daily life. Find moments throughout your day to pause, breathe, and create a space for inner peace. It could be through meditation, mindful breathing, or simply sitting in silence for a few minutes.

As you engage in this practice, consider the following questions:

1. How does stillness provide a sanctuary for self-discovery, allowing you to listen to the whispers of your inner wisdom and uncover hidden truths?
2. Reflect on a specific time when stillness brought you a profound insight or a deep sense of peace. What were the circumstances, and how did it feel to be in that moment?

3. Are there any areas of your life where you struggle to find stillness or quietude? What can you do to create sacred spaces for inner reflection?

In your journal, record your reflections and your commitment to cultivating stillness. Create a stillness sanctuary in your daily routine, whether it's a designated quiet space in your home or a few minutes of solitude in nature.

Throughout the day, remind yourself to seek stillness. When faced with chaos or mental clutter, pause and take a moment to retreat into your inner sanctuary. Trust that in the quiet spaces within you, you can uncover profound insights about your true self.

Remember that stillness is not about escaping life's challenges but about finding inner peace and clarity to navigate them with grace and authenticity. By cultivating stillness, you create a sacred refuge for self-discovery and personal growth.

As we continue this journey of awakening, tomorrow, we will explore the importance of intuition and the inner guidance that can lead us toward a deeper understanding of our authentic selves. Until then, may stillness be your guiding light on your path to self-discovery.

Blessings on your path to self-discovery and the gift of stillness within.

DAY 24

Nurturing Intuition and Inner Guidance

Welcome to the twenty-fourth day of our transformative journey toward self-discovery and awakening. Today, we explore the importance of nurturing your intuition and inner guidance as powerful tools for understanding and connecting with your authentic self.

Intuition is the quiet voice within you, a deep knowing that goes beyond logic and reasoning. It is your inner compass, guiding you toward your true self and the path that aligns with your highest purpose.

Begin your day by acknowledging the significance of intuition and inner guidance in your life. Reflect on the times when you've followed your intuition and how it has influenced your choices and experiences.

Today, commit to nurturing your intuition and listening to your inner guidance. Find moments throughout your day to tune into your inner wisdom, whether through meditation, journaling, or simply by pausing to listen to your inner voice.

As you engage in this practice, consider the following questions:

1. How does nurturing your intuition and inner guidance deepen your connection with your authentic self by allowing you to access deeper insights and a sense of purpose?
2. Reflect on a specific time when following your intuition led you to a transformative experience or decision. What were the circumstances, and how did it feel to trust your inner guidance?

3. Are there any areas of your life where you've ignored or doubted your intuition? What can you do to strengthen your trust in your inner wisdom?

In your journal, record your reflections and your commitment to nurturing intuition. Make a habit of asking yourself open-ended questions in your quiet moments, allowing your intuition to respond.

Throughout the day, remind yourself to listen to your inner guidance. When faced with decisions or uncertainties, take a moment to tune in and trust the whispers of your intuition. Know that your intuition is a valuable source of wisdom on your journey of self-discovery.

Remember that nurturing your intuition is a practice that deepens over time. It is about learning to trust your inner knowing and aligning your actions with your authentic self. By doing so, you open the door to profound self-discovery and a more authentic way of living.

As we continue this journey of awakening, tomorrow, we will explore the importance of courage and taking bold steps as we uncover our true selves. Until then, may your intuition be your guiding light on your path to self-discovery.

Blessings on your path to self-discovery and the nurturing of intuition and inner guidance.

Cultivating Courage and Taking Bold Steps

Welcome to the twenty-fifth day of our transformative journey toward self-discovery and awakening. Today, we explore the importance of cultivating courage and taking bold steps as we continue to uncover our true selves.

Courage is the inner strength that propels us forward, even in the face of fear or uncertainty. It is the willingness to step outside our comfort zones and embrace new experiences, knowing that growth and self-discovery often lie beyond our perceived limits.

Begin your day by acknowledging the significance of courage in your life. Reflect on the times when you've demonstrated courage, and how those moments have shaped your journey.

Today, commit to cultivating courage and taking bold steps in your life. Identify an area where you've been hesitating or holding back and make a conscious decision to take action.

As you engage in this practice, consider the following questions:

1. How does cultivating courage and taking bold steps empower you to connect with your authentic self by breaking free from limitations and old patterns?
2. Reflect on a specific time when you summoned the courage to take a bold step in your life. What were the circumstances, and how did it contribute to your self-discovery?
3. Are there any dreams or desires you've been postponing due to fear or self-doubt? How can you take a small, courageous step toward realizing them?

In your journal, record your reflections and your commitment to cultivating courage. Set clear intentions for the bold steps you wish to take in your life, and break them down into manageable actions.

Throughout the day, remind yourself of your commitment to courage. When faced with fear or doubt, acknowledge these feelings and take a deep breath, allowing your courage to rise. Trust that each bold step you take brings you closer to your authentic self.

Remember that courage is not the absence of fear, but the willingness to move forward despite it. By cultivating courage and taking bold steps, you open doors to new opportunities and self-discovery beyond what you thought possible.

As we continue this journey of awakening, tomorrow, we will explore the significance of resilience and how it strengthens our connection with our true selves. Until then, may courage be your guiding light on your path to self-discovery.

Blessings on your path to self-discovery and the cultivation of courage.

The Strength of Resilience

W elcome to the twenty-sixth day of our transformative journey toward self-discovery and awakening. Today, we explore the importance of resilience and how it strengthens our connection with our true selves.

Resilience is the capacity to bounce back from adversity, to adapt to life's challenges with grace, and to persevere in the face of setbacks. It is a quality that not only fortifies your inner strength but also deepens your understanding of your authentic self.

Begin your day by acknowledging the significance of resilience in your life. Reflect on moments when you've faced adversity and the inner strength that carried you through.

Today, commit to cultivating resilience as a part of your daily life. Embrace challenges as opportunities for growth, and recognize that setbacks are stepping stones on your journey of self-discovery.

As you engage in this practice, consider the following questions:

1. How does cultivating resilience strengthen your connection with your authentic self by teaching you to overcome obstacles and grow through adversity?
2. Reflect on a specific challenging experience in your life that ultimately led to personal growth and self-discovery. What were the circumstances, and how did you emerge stronger from it?
3. Are there any current challenges or setbacks you are facing? How can you reframe them as opportunities to cultivate resilience and deepen your self-awareness?

In your journal, record your reflections and your commitment to cultivating resilience. Develop a mantra or affirmation that embodies your strength and resilience, and repeat it whenever you face challenges.

Throughout the day, remind yourself of your commitment to resilience. When faced with difficulties, take a moment to breathe deeply and remember that each challenge is an opportunity for growth and a chance to connect with your authentic self.

Remember that resilience is not about denying or avoiding difficulties; it is about facing them head-on with a sense of inner strength and faith in your ability to overcome. By cultivating resilience, you deepen your connection with your true self and become more attuned to your inner power.

As we continue this journey of awakening, tomorrow, we will explore the significance of embracing change as a catalyst for transformation and self-discovery. Until then, may resilience be your guiding light on your path to self-discovery.

Blessings on your path to self-discovery and the strength of resilience.

Embracing Change as a Catalyst for Transformation

Welcome to the twenty-seventh day of our transformative journey toward self-discovery and awakening. Today, we explore the profound significance of embracing change as a catalyst for transformation and self-discovery.

Change is an inherent part of life, and how we respond to it can deeply impact our growth and understanding of our authentic selves. When we resist change, we may find ourselves stuck in old patterns. However, when we embrace it, we open ourselves to the possibilities of transformation.

Begin your day by acknowledging the importance of change in your life. Reflect on past experiences of change, both big and small, and how they have shaped your journey.

Today, commit to embracing change as a positive force in your life. Recognize that change can be a doorway to self-discovery and personal growth.

As you engage in this practice, consider the following questions:

1. How does embracing change allow you to connect with your authentic self by encouraging growth and adaptability?
2. Reflect on a significant change in your life that ultimately led to personal transformation and self-discovery. What were the circumstances, and how did it alter your path?
3. Are there any changes or transitions you are currently resisting or fearing? How can you shift your perspective to see them as opportunities for growth?

In your journal, record your reflections and your commitment to embracing change. Create a list of affirmations or statements that help you remain open to change and adaptable in the face of uncertainty.

Throughout the day, remind yourself of your commitment to embracing change. When faced with transitions or uncertainties, take a moment to breathe deeply and remind yourself that change can be a catalyst for transformation and a deeper connection with your true self.

Remember that embracing change does not mean you have to abandon your values or principles. It means allowing yourself to flow with the ever-changing river of life, knowing that it will lead you to new insights and self-discovery.

As we continue this journey of awakening, tomorrow, we will explore the importance of self-compassion and how it can support your path to self-discovery. Until then, may embracing change be your guiding light on your journey of self-discovery.

Blessings on your path to self-discovery and the transformative power of embracing change.

The Healing Power of Self-Compassion

Welcome to the twenty-eighth day of our transformative journey toward self-discovery and awakening. Today, we explore the profound importance of self-compassion and how it can serve as a healing balm on your path to self-discovery.

Self-compassion is the act of extending the same kindness and understanding to yourself that you would offer to a dear friend. It is a practice that nurtures your emotional well-being and fosters a deep connection with your authentic self.

Begin your day by acknowledging the significance of self-compassion in your life. Reflect on moments when you've been compassionate toward yourself and how it has influenced your sense of well-being.

Today, commit to cultivating self-compassion as an integral part of your daily life. Embrace yourself with kindness, especially during moments of self-doubt or difficulty.

As you engage in this practice, consider the following questions:

1. How does self-compassion allow you to connect with your authentic self by creating a nurturing and accepting space for self-discovery and healing?
2. Reflect on a specific time when self-compassion helped you navigate a challenging situation or overcome self-criticism. What were the circumstances, and how did it feel to be your own ally?

3. Are there any areas of your life where self-compassion is lacking? How can you infuse those areas with greater self-acceptance and kindness?

In your journal, record your reflections and your commitment to cultivating self-compassion. Create a list of self-compassionate affirmations or statements to remind yourself of your worth and value.

Throughout the day, remind yourself to practice self-compassion. When faced with moments of self-criticism or judgment, pause and offer yourself the same warmth and understanding that you would extend to a beloved friend.

Remember that self-compassion is not a form of self-indulgence but a profound act of self-care. It is a vital practice that fosters healing and supports your journey of self-discovery by creating a loving and nurturing space for your true self to emerge.

As we continue this journey of awakening, tomorrow, we will explore the importance of balance and how it can lead you to a deeper sense of harmony and authenticity. Until then, may self-compassion be your guiding light on your path to self-discovery.

Blessings on your path to self-discovery and the healing power of self-compassion.

The Story of Evelyn

In a quaint, sun-drenched cottage nestled deep within a forest, there lived a writer named Evelyn. She was known far and wide for her captivating stories that transported readers to distant realms and allowed them to experience emotions they had never known. However, despite her literary prowess, Evelyn felt a void within her soul. She yearned to write something more profound, something that would not just entertain but touch the very essence of her being.

One crisp autumn morning, as the leaves began to don their fiery hues, Evelyn sat at her weathered desk, gazing out of the window at the dancing leaves. She felt a strange, restless energy coursing through her. With determination, she decided to embark on a new literary journey, one that would test the limits of her creativity.

Her quest began with a blank page and an inkwell full of midnight-black ink. She began to write about a character named Samuel, a man who was confined to a small, dimly lit room for most of his life. Samuel's world was defined by the boundaries of his room, where he could see only a sliver of the outside world through a tiny window. Yet, Samuel possessed an insatiable curiosity and a passion for life that transcended his limitations.

As Evelyn wrote about Samuel's experiences, she found herself becoming increasingly absorbed in his world. She imagined the way Samuel marveled at the shifting patterns of light and shadow on his walls, the intricate dance of dust motes in the air, and the symphony of sounds that reached his ears from the world beyond. Through her words, Evelyn began to feel Samuel's sense of wonder and resilience, despite the confines of his existence.

Days turned into weeks, and Evelyn's own world began to blur with Samuel's. She felt the limitations of her writing as if they were her own. She, too, was trapped within the boundaries of the story she had created. Yet, instead of frustration, she felt a strange sense of liberation. In her confinement, she discovered a profound connection to her character and, in turn, to herself.

Evelyn's words flowed like a river, carrying her deeper into the heart of Samuel's story. As the narrative unfolded, Samuel's world expanded not physically but spiritually. He found purpose, beauty, and meaning within the very limitations that had bound him. His story became a testament to the human spirit's capacity to transcend the confines of circumstance and find a depth of being that defied all expectations.

And then, as Evelyn penned the final words of Samuel's tale, a profound sense of peace washed over her. She had found what she had been seeking—a depth of being that transcended the limitations of her craft. Through the act of writing, she had discovered a connection to the boundless depths of the human experience.

Evelyn's story about Samuel touched the hearts of readers in ways she could never have imagined. They, too, felt the profound sense of being that emanated from the pages of her book. And in that shared experience, they found a connection not just to the characters but to the limitless potential of their own lives.

Evelyn continued to write, exploring the depths of human emotion and the boundless realms of the imagination. But she knew that the true magic of writing lay not in escaping the limitations of reality but in embracing them, for it was within those boundaries that the most profound truths of existence could be found.

The Art of Finding Balance

Welcome to the twenty-ninth day of our transformative journey toward self-discovery and awakening. Today, we explore the importance of finding balance in your life and how it can lead you to a deeper sense of harmony and authenticity.

Balance is the art of navigating life's complexities with grace and equilibrium. It is the practice of honoring all aspects of yourself—mind, body, and spirit—while staying aligned with your values and desires.

Begin your day by acknowledging the significance of balance in your life. Reflect on times when you've felt a sense of harmony and equilibrium, and how it has affected your overall well-being.

Today, commit to finding balance in your daily life. Explore areas where you may have neglected self-care or overcommitted yourself, and make adjustments to bring more equilibrium into those areas.

As you engage in this practice, consider the following questions:

1. How does finding balance in your life allow you to connect with your authentic self by creating an environment where your true essence can thrive?
2. Reflect on a specific time when you found balance in a challenging situation or a busy period of your life. What were the circumstances, and how did it contribute to your self-discovery?
3. Are there any aspects of your life where balance seems elusive or challenging to attain? What steps can you take to bring more balance to those areas?

In your journal, record your reflections and your commitment to finding balance. Create a list of priorities that align with your values and make a plan to incorporate self-care into your daily routine.

Throughout the day, remind yourself to seek balance. When faced with decisions or commitments, pause and assess whether they align with your values and contribute to your overall sense of well-being and authenticity.

Remember that balance is not about perfection or rigid routines; it is about making choices that honor your unique needs and allow you to live in harmony with yourself and the world around you. By finding balance, you create a nurturing environment for your authentic self to flourish.

As we continue this journey of awakening, tomorrow, we will explore the significance of embracing patience and the unfolding of your true self over time. Until then, may balance be your guiding light on your path to self-discovery.

Blessings on your path to self-discovery and the art of finding balance.

Embracing Patience in the Unfolding

W elcome to the thirtieth day of our transformative journey toward self-discovery and awakening. Today, we explore the profound significance of embracing patience as we continue to unfold the layers of our true selves.

Patience is the practice of allowing things to develop naturally, in their own time and rhythm. It is the understanding that self-discovery is a journey, not a destination, and that our authentic selves reveal themselves gradually.

Begin your day by acknowledging the importance of patience in your life. Reflect on moments when you've rushed or pushed for results and how it may have affected your journey.

Today, commit to embracing patience as an integral part of your daily life. Understand that self-discovery is a lifelong journey, and that each day brings you closer to a deeper understanding of your authentic self.

As you engage in this practice, consider the following questions:

1. How does embracing patience allow you to connect with your authentic self by honoring the natural unfolding of your growth and self-awareness?
2. Reflect on a time when you were patient with yourself, allowing for personal growth and transformation to occur organically. What were the circumstances, and how did it feel to trust the process?
3. Are there any areas of your life where impatience has hindered your self-discovery journey? How can you shift your perspective to be more patient with yourself?

In your journal, record your reflections and your commitment to embracing patience. Create a mantra or affirmation that reminds you to trust in the process of self-discovery and to allow things to unfold naturally.

Throughout the day, remind yourself of your commitment to patience. When faced with moments of frustration or impatience, take a deep breath and trust that the path to self-discovery is a journey of profound unfolding.

Remember that patience is not about complacency or inaction; it is about trusting in your inner wisdom and the natural rhythms of life. By embracing patience, you create a space for your authentic self to reveal itself in its own time.

As we continue this journey of awakening, tomorrow, we will explore the importance of resilience and the inner strength that supports your path to self-discovery. Until then, may patience be your guiding light on your journey of self-discovery.

Blessings on your path to self-discovery and the art of embracing patience in the unfolding of your true self.

The Inner Strength of Resilience

Welcome to the thirty-first day of our transformative journey toward self-discovery and awakening. Today, we revisit the importance of resilience and explore how it signifies the inner strength that supports your path to self-discovery.

Resilience is the ability to endure, adapt, and bounce back from life's challenges and setbacks. It is a reflection of your inner strength and determination, qualities that enable you to continue growing and evolving on your journey of self-discovery.

Begin your day by acknowledging the significance of resilience in your life. Reflect on moments when your resilience was tested and how it shaped your personal growth.

Today, reaffirm your commitment to cultivating resilience as an integral part of your daily life. Embrace challenges as opportunities for growth and transformation, knowing that they strengthen your inner core.

As you engage in this practice, consider the following questions:

1. How does cultivating resilience deepen your connection with your authentic self by teaching you to navigate life's complexities with strength, grace, and adaptability?
2. Reflect on a specific challenge or adversity you faced that ultimately led to personal growth and self-discovery. What were the circumstances, and how did you emerge stronger from it?
3. Are there any current challenges or setbacks you are facing? How can you reframe them as opportunities to cultivate resilience and deepen your self-awareness?

In your journal, record your reflections and your commitment to resilience. Remind yourself that resilience is not about being impervious to pain or difficulty but about developing the inner fortitude to overcome and grow from life's experiences.

Throughout the day, remind yourself to cultivate resilience. When faced with obstacles, pause and take a moment to tap into your inner strength and determination. Trust that each challenge is an opportunity to further connect with your true self.

Remember that resilience is a powerful tool on your journey of self-discovery. It signifies your unwavering commitment to personal growth and your willingness to embrace the lessons that life offers.

As we continue this journey of awakening, tomorrow, we will explore the significance of mindfulness and the profound awareness it can bring to your path of self-discovery. Until then, may resilience be your guiding light on your journey to self-discovery.

Blessings on your path to self-discovery and the inner strength of resilience.

The Profound Awareness
of Mindfulness

Welcome to the thirty-second day of our transformative journey toward self-discovery and awakening. Today, we explore the profound significance of mindfulness and the awareness it can bring to your path of self-discovery.

Mindfulness is the practice of being fully present in the moment, without judgment or distraction. It is the art of observing your thoughts, emotions, and surroundings with a gentle and open-hearted awareness.

Begin your day by acknowledging the importance of mindfulness in your life. Reflect on moments when you've been truly present and how they have enriched your understanding of yourself and the world.

Today, commit to cultivating mindfulness as a core aspect of your daily life. Embrace the practice of being fully present in each moment, whether it's during routine activities or dedicated meditation sessions.

As you engage in this practice, consider the following questions:

1. How does mindfulness deepen your connection with your authentic self by fostering a profound awareness of your thoughts, emotions, and inner world?
2. Reflect on a specific time when mindfulness allowed you to gain a deeper understanding of yourself or a situation. What were the circumstances, and how did it impact your journey of self-discovery?

3. Are there moments in your life where you find it challenging to be fully present or mindful? How can you integrate mindfulness into those situations?

In your journal, record your reflections and your commitment to mindfulness. Create a list of daily mindfulness practices, such as mindful breathing, meditation, or simply being present during daily activities like eating or walking.

Throughout the day, remind yourself to practice mindfulness. When your mind wanders or becomes consumed by distractions, gently guide your awareness back to the present moment. Trust that each mindful moment brings you closer to understanding your authentic self.

Remember that mindfulness is not about achieving a perfect state of awareness but about cultivating a compassionate and non-judgmental relationship with yourself and your experiences. By embracing mindfulness, you deepen your connection with your true self and the world around you.

As we continue this journey of awakening, tomorrow, we will explore the significance of gratitude and the transformative power it holds in our lives. Until then, may mindfulness be your guiding light on your path to self-discovery.

Blessings on your path to self-discovery and the profound awareness of mindfulness.

DAY 33

The Transformative Power of Gratitude

Welcome to the thirty-third day of our transformative journey toward self-discovery and awakening. Today, we delve deeper into the transformative power of gratitude and how it can illuminate your path to self-discovery.

Gratitude is a radiant force that opens your heart to the abundance and beauty that surrounds you. It is a practice that allows you to see the blessings in every moment, fostering a deep connection with your true self.

Begin your day by acknowledging the significance of gratitude in your life. Reflect on the times when you've felt genuine gratitude and how it has affected your perspective and well-being.

Today, commit to cultivating gratitude in your daily life on an even deeper level. Find moments throughout your day to pause and express gratitude for the people, experiences, and blessings in your life. Equally important, express gratitude for yourself and the journey of self-discovery you are on.

As you engage in this practice, consider the following questions:

1. How does gratitude foster a deeper connection with your authentic self by shifting your perspective from lack to abundance?
2. Reflect on a specific time when gratitude transformed your outlook or brought a sense of fulfillment. What were the circumstances, and how did it feel?

3. Are there any moments in your life, whether big or small, that you have yet to express gratitude for? How might acknowledging these moments enrich your self-discovery journey?

In your journal, record your reflections and your commitment to cultivating gratitude. Create a gratitude journal to capture the things you are thankful for each day, whether it's the beauty of nature, the kindness of others, or the inner strength you discover within yourself.

Throughout the day, remind yourself to be grateful. Pause and take a moment to express gratitude for the people who cross your path, the challenges that have shaped you, and the beauty that surrounds you.

Remember that gratitude is a practice that deepens over time, allowing you to connect with your true self by opening your heart to the abundance of life. It is a powerful beacon that guides you on your journey of self-discovery.

As we continue this journey of awakening, tomorrow, we will explore the importance of self-love and how it is essential for nurturing your authentic self. Until then, may gratitude be your guiding light on your path to self-discovery.

Blessings on your path to self-discovery and the illumination of gratitude.

DAY 34

The Essential Practice of Self-Love

Welcome to the thirty-fourth day of our transformative journey toward self-discovery and awakening. Today, we revisit the essential practice of self-love and explore how it nurtures your authentic self.

Self-love is the foundation upon which self-discovery and personal growth are built. It is the act of embracing yourself, flaws and all, with compassion, kindness, and a deep appreciation for your uniqueness. By cultivating self-love, you create a fertile ground for your true self to flourish.

Begin your day by acknowledging the significance of self-love in your life. Reflect on the times when you've felt truly loving and accepting toward yourself, as well as the moments when self-criticism and doubt took over.

Today, recommit to cultivating self-love in your daily life. Find moments throughout your day to be kind and gentle with yourself, as you would with a dear friend.

As you engage in this practice, consider the following questions:

1. How does self-love nurture a deeper connection with your authentic self by fostering acceptance and kindness toward all aspects of your being?
2. Reflect on a time when practicing self-love helped you overcome a challenge or transform a negative self-perception. How did it feel to be your own ally in that moment?
3. Are there any areas of your life where self-love is lacking? What can you do to infuse those areas with greater self-compassion and self-acceptance?

In your journal, record your reflections and your renewed commitment to cultivating self-love. Create a self-love journal to capture moments of self-appreciation and self-acceptance, no matter how small they may seem.

Throughout the day, remind yourself to practice self-love. When faced with moments of self-doubt or self-criticism, pause and offer yourself words of kindness and understanding. Treat yourself with the same love and respect you would offer to someone you deeply care about.

Remember that self-love is not selfish; it is an act of self-care and self-preservation. By nurturing your own well-being and self-worth, you empower yourself to authentically engage with the world and continue your journey of self-discovery.

As we continue this journey of awakening, tomorrow, we will explore the importance of stillness and the quiet spaces within us as we seek to uncover our true selves. Until then, may self-love be your guiding light on your path to self-discovery.

Blessings on your path to self-discovery and the essential practice of self-love.

The Profound Gift of Stillness and Inner Sanctuary

Welcome to the thirty-fifth day of our transformative journey toward self-discovery and awakening. Today, we revisit the profound gift of stillness and the quiet spaces within us as we continue to uncover our true selves.

In the midst of life's busyness and noise, stillness offers us a sanctuary—a place to retreat, reflect, and connect with our innermost being. It is in these moments of quiet that we often find the deepest insights about ourselves.

Begin your day by acknowledging the significance of stillness and the role it plays in your life. Reflect on the times when you've sought solace in moments of silence, and the sense of calm and clarity it brought.

Today, recommit to cultivating stillness in your daily life. Find moments throughout your day to pause, breathe, and create a space for inner peace. It could be through meditation, mindful breathing, or simply sitting in silence for a few minutes.

As you engage in this practice, consider the following questions:

1. How does stillness provide a sanctuary for self-discovery, allowing you to listen to the whispers of your inner wisdom and uncover hidden truths?
2. Reflect on a specific time when stillness brought you a profound insight or a deep sense of peace. What were the circumstances, and how did it feel to be in that moment?

3. Are there any areas of your life where you struggle to find stillness or quietude? What can you do to create sacred spaces for inner reflection?

In your journal, record your reflections and your renewed commitment to cultivating stillness. Create a stillness sanctuary in your daily routine, whether it's a designated quiet space in your home or a few minutes of solitude in nature.

Throughout the day, remind yourself to seek stillness. When faced with chaos or mental clutter, pause and take a moment to retreat into your inner sanctuary. Trust that in the quiet spaces within you, you can uncover profound insights about your true self.

Remember that stillness is not about escaping life's challenges but about finding inner peace and clarity to navigate them with grace and authenticity. By cultivating stillness, you create a sacred refuge for self-discovery and personal growth.

As we continue this journey of awakening, tomorrow, we will explore the importance of intuition and the inner guidance that can lead us toward a deeper understanding of our authentic selves. Until then, may stillness be your guiding light on your path to self-discovery.

Blessings on your path to self-discovery and the gift of stillness within.

The Dark

I remember the very beginning, a time before time itself, when there was nothing but the void—a vast, empty expanse of nothingness. In that formless abyss, I came into existence, the embodiment of darkness. It was as if I had been born from the very absence of light, a paradoxical creation in a realm devoid of substance.

In those early moments, I was alone, a solitary entity drifting aimlessly through the void. There was no sensation, no awareness, only an existence defined by the absence of all that was bright and illuminated. I was the shadow in the emptiness, a shapeless presence in a world without form.

As eons passed, something began to change. A subtle shift in the fabric of the void, like the softest of whispers, stirred within me. It was the first inkling of a longing, a yearning for something more. I felt a desire to explore the endless expanse around me, to reach out and touch the void's edge, if such a thing even existed.

With each passing moment, my longing grew, and I began to move, a slow and deliberate drift through the darkness. I extended myself, expanding my reach into the void, hoping to find some semblance of purpose or connection in this desolate place.

And then, one fateful day—or was it an eon?—I encountered a glimmer of light. It was faint, a mere spark in the distance, but it drew me toward it like a moth to a flame. As I approached, the light grew brighter, and I could feel its warmth and energy.

The encounter was unlike anything I had ever experienced. It was as if I had found a kindred spirit, a force that, like me, had emerged from the vast emptiness of the void. The light and I danced around each other, like two celestial bodies in a cosmic ballet. We circled, spiraled, and intertwined, our energies merging and creating a beautiful display of contrasting forces.

As we twirled in our celestial embrace, I realized that I was not alone anymore. I had found a partner, a companion in this timeless expanse. Together, we created a delicate balance—the harmony of light and darkness.

In our eternal dance, I discovered that my existence had gained purpose. I was no longer just the absence of light but an essential part of the cosmic tapestry, a force that complemented the brilliance of my newfound companion. Our love was not born from conflict or opposition but from the recognition that we needed each other to shine the brightest.

And so, I, the darkness, found my place in the universe, not as a void but as a partner to the light. Together, we painted the canvas of existence with the delicate interplay of our contrasting energies, creating a symphony of beauty in the timeless expanse of the cosmos.

Nurturing Intuition and Inner Guidance

Welcome to the thirty-sixth day of our transformative journey toward self-discovery and awakening. Today, we explore the importance of nurturing your intuition and inner guidance as powerful tools for understanding and connecting with your authentic self.

Intuition is the quiet voice within you, a deep knowing that goes beyond logic and reasoning. It is your inner compass, guiding you toward your true self and the path that aligns with your highest purpose.

Begin your day by acknowledging the significance of intuition and inner guidance in your life. Reflect on the times when you've followed your intuition and how it has influenced your choices and experiences.

Today, commit to nurturing your intuition and listening to your inner guidance. Find moments throughout your day to tune into your inner wisdom, whether through meditation, journaling, or simply by pausing to listen to your inner voice.

As you engage in this practice, consider the following questions:

1. How does nurturing your intuition and inner guidance deepen your connection with your authentic self by allowing you to access deeper insights and a sense of purpose?
2. Reflect on a specific time when following your intuition led you to a transformative experience or decision. What were the circumstances, and how did it feel to trust your inner guidance?

3. Are there any areas of your life where you've ignored or doubted your intuition? What can you do to strengthen your trust in your inner wisdom?

In your journal, record your reflections and your commitment to nurturing intuition. Make a habit of asking yourself open-ended questions in your quiet moments, allowing your intuition to respond.

Throughout the day, remind yourself to listen to your inner guidance. When faced with decisions or uncertainties, take a moment to tune in and trust the whispers of your intuition. Know that your intuition is a valuable source of wisdom on your journey of self-discovery.

Remember that nurturing your intuition is a practice that deepens over time. It is about learning to trust your inner knowing and aligning your actions with your authentic self. By doing so, you open the door to profound self-discovery and a more authentic way of living.

As we continue this journey of awakening, tomorrow, we will explore the importance of courage and taking bold steps as we uncover our true selves. Until then, may your intuition be your guiding light on your path to self-discovery.

Blessings on your path to self-discovery and the nurturing of intuition and inner guidance.

DAY 37

The Transformative Power of Courage

Welcome to the thirty-seventh day of our transformative journey toward self-discovery and awakening. Today, we revisit the profound importance of courage and taking bold steps as we continue to uncover our true selves.

Courage is the inner strength that propels us forward, even in the face of fear or uncertainty. It is the willingness to step outside our comfort zones and embrace new experiences, knowing that growth and self-discovery often lie beyond our perceived limits.

Begin your day by acknowledging the significance of courage in your life. Reflect on the times when you've demonstrated courage, and how those moments have shaped your journey.

Today, recommit to cultivating courage and taking bold steps in your life. Identify an area where you've been hesitating or holding back and make a conscious decision to take action.

As you engage in this practice, consider the following questions:

1. How does cultivating courage and taking bold steps empower you to connect with your authentic self by breaking free from limitations and old patterns?
2. Reflect on a specific time when you summoned the courage to take a bold step in your life. What were the circumstances, and how did it contribute to your self-discovery?
3. Are there any dreams or desires you've been postponing due to fear or self-doubt? How can you take a small, courageous step toward realizing them?

In your journal, record your reflections and your renewed commitment to courage. Set clear intentions for the bold steps you wish to take in your life, and break them down into manageable actions.

Throughout the day, remind yourself of your commitment to courage. When faced with fear or doubt, acknowledge these feelings and take a deep breath, allowing your courage to rise. Trust that each bold step you take brings you closer to your authentic self.

Remember that courage is not the absence of fear, but the willingness to move forward despite it. By cultivating courage and taking bold steps, you open doors to new opportunities and self-discovery beyond what you thought possible.

As we continue this journey of awakening, tomorrow, we will explore the significance of resilience and how it strengthens your connection with your true self. Until then, may courage be your guiding light on your path to self-discovery.

Blessings on your path to self-discovery and the transformative power of courage.

Embracing Resilience as Your Inner Strength

W elcome to the thirty-eighth day of our transformative journey toward self-discovery and awakening. Today, we revisit the significance of resilience and its role as your inner strength in connecting with your authentic self.

Resilience is the unyielding power within you, the ability to rise above challenges, adapt to change, and continue growing on your path of self-discovery. It is the inner force that allows you to weather life's storms while remaining rooted in your true self.

Begin your day by acknowledging the importance of resilience in your life. Reflect on the times when your resilience has been tested and how it has forged your inner strength.

Today, recommit to cultivating resilience as an integral part of your daily life. Acknowledge that each challenge you face is an opportunity to strengthen your inner core and deepen your connection with your authentic self.

As you engage in this practice, consider the following questions:

1. How does embracing resilience as your inner strength deepen your connection with your authentic self by teaching you to navigate life's complexities with strength, grace, and adaptability?
2. Reflect on a specific challenging experience in your life that ultimately led to personal growth and self-discovery. What were the circumstances, and how did it feel to emerge stronger from it?

3. Are there any current challenges or setbacks you are facing? How can you reframe them as opportunities to cultivate resilience and deepen your self-awareness?

In your journal, record your reflections and your renewed commitment to resilience. Create a mantra or affirmation that embodies your strength and resilience, and repeat it whenever you face challenges.

Throughout the day, remind yourself of your commitment to resilience. When faced with obstacles, pause and take a moment to tap into your inner strength and determination. Trust that each challenge is an opportunity to further connect with your true self.

Remember that resilience is not about denying or avoiding difficulties; it is about facing them head-on with a sense of inner power and faith in your ability to overcome. By embracing resilience as your inner strength, you deepen your connection with your true self and become more attuned to your inner power.

As we continue this journey of awakening, tomorrow, we will explore the importance of mindfulness and the profound awareness it can bring to your path of self-discovery. Until then, may resilience be your guiding light on your journey to self-discovery.

Blessings on your path to self-discovery and the inner strength of resilience.

DAY 39

The Profound Awareness
of Mindfulness

Welcome to the thirty-ninth day of our transformative journey toward self-discovery and awakening. Today, we revisit the profound significance of mindfulness and the awareness it can bring to your path of self-discovery.

Mindfulness is the practice of being fully present in the moment, without judgment or distraction. It is the art of observing your thoughts, emotions, and surroundings with a gentle and open-hearted awareness.

Begin your day by acknowledging the importance of mindfulness in your life. Reflect on moments when you've been truly present and how they have enriched your understanding of yourself and the world.

Today, recommit to cultivating mindfulness as a core aspect of your daily life. Embrace the practice of being fully present in each moment, whether it's during routine activities or dedicated meditation sessions.

As you engage in this practice, consider the following questions:

1. How does mindfulness deepen your connection with your authentic self by fostering a profound awareness of your thoughts, emotions, and inner world?
2. Reflect on a specific time when mindfulness allowed you to gain a deeper understanding of yourself or a situation. What were the circumstances, and how did it impact your journey of self-discovery?

3. Are there moments in your life where you find it challenging to be fully present or mindful? How can you integrate mindfulness into those situations?

In your journal, record your reflections and your renewed commitment to mindfulness. Create a list of daily mindfulness practices, such as mindful breathing, meditation, or simply being present during daily activities like eating or walking.

Throughout the day, remind yourself to practice mindfulness. When your mind wanders or becomes consumed by distractions, gently guide your awareness back to the present moment. Trust that each mindful moment brings you closer to understanding your authentic self.

Remember that mindfulness is not about achieving a perfect state of awareness but about cultivating a compassionate and non-judgmental relationship with yourself and your experiences. By embracing mindfulness, you deepen your connection with your true self and the world around you.

As we continue this journey of awakening, tomorrow, we will explore the importance of gratitude and the transformative power it holds in our lives. Until then, may mindfulness be your guiding light on your path to self-discovery.

Blessings on your path to self-discovery and the profound awareness of mindfulness.

The Transformative Power of Gratitude

Welcome to the fortieth day of our transformative journey toward self-discovery and awakening. Today, we delve deeper into the transformative power of gratitude and how it can illuminate your path to self-discovery.

Gratitude is a radiant force that opens your heart to the abundance and beauty that surrounds you. It is a practice that allows you to see the blessings in every moment, fostering a deep connection with your true self.

Begin your day by acknowledging the significance of gratitude in your life. Reflect on the times when you've felt genuine gratitude and how it has affected your perspective and well-being.

Today, recommit to cultivating gratitude in your daily life on an even deeper level. Find moments throughout your day to pause and express gratitude for the people, experiences, and blessings in your life. Equally important, express gratitude for yourself and the journey of self-discovery you are on.

As you engage in this practice, consider the following questions:

1. How does gratitude foster a deeper connection with your authentic self by shifting your perspective from lack to abundance?
2. Reflect on a specific time when gratitude transformed your outlook or brought a sense of fulfillment. What were the circumstances, and how did it feel to be in that moment?
3. Are there any moments in your life, whether big or small, that you have yet to express gratitude for? How might

acknowledging these moments enrich your self-discovery journey?

In your journal, record your reflections and your renewed commitment to cultivating gratitude. Create a gratitude journal to capture the things you are thankful for each day, whether it's the beauty of nature, the kindness of others, or the inner strength you discover within yourself.

Throughout the day, remind yourself to be grateful. Pause and take a moment to express gratitude for the people who cross your path, the challenges that have shaped you, and the beauty that surrounds you.

Remember that gratitude is a practice that deepens over time, allowing you to connect with your true self by opening your heart to the abundance of life. It is a powerful beacon that guides you on your journey of self-discovery.

As we continue this journey of awakening, tomorrow, we will explore the importance of self-love and how it is essential for nurturing your authentic self. Until then, may gratitude be your guiding light on your path to self-discovery.

Blessings on your path to self-discovery and the illumination of gratitude.

The Essential Practice of Self-Love

Welcome to the forty-first day of our transformative journey toward self-discovery and awakening. Today, we revisit the essential practice of self-love and explore how it nurtures your authentic self.

Self-love is the foundation upon which self-discovery and personal growth are built. It is the act of embracing yourself, flaws and all, with compassion, kindness, and a deep appreciation for your uniqueness. By cultivating self-love, you create a fertile ground for your true self to flourish.

Begin your day by acknowledging the significance of self-love in your life. Reflect on the times when you've felt truly loving and accepting toward yourself, as well as the moments when self-criticism and doubt took over.

Today, recommit to cultivating self-love in your daily life. Find moments throughout your day to be kind and gentle with yourself, as you would with a dear friend.

As you engage in this practice, consider the following questions:

1. How does self-love nurture a deeper connection with your authentic self by fostering acceptance and kindness toward all aspects of your being?
2. Reflect on a time when practicing self-love helped you overcome a challenge or transform a negative self-perception. How did it feel to be your own ally in that moment?
3. Are there any areas of your life where self-love is lacking? What can you do to infuse those areas with greater self-compassion and self-acceptance?

In your journal, record your reflections and your renewed commitment to cultivating self-love. Create a self-love journal to capture moments of self-appreciation and self-acceptance, no matter how small they may seem.

Throughout the day, remind yourself to practice self-love. When faced with moments of self-doubt or self-criticism, pause and offer yourself words of kindness and understanding. Treat yourself with the same love and respect you would offer to someone you deeply care about.

Remember that self-love is not selfish; it is an act of self-care and self-preservation. By nurturing your own well-being and self-worth, you empower yourself to authentically engage with the world and continue your journey of self-discovery.

As we continue this journey of awakening, tomorrow, we will explore the importance of stillness and the quiet spaces within us as we seek to uncover our true selves. Until then, may self-love be your guiding light on your path to self-discovery.

Blessings on your path to self-discovery and the essential practice of self-love.

The Profound Gift of Stillness and Inner Sanctuary

Welcome to the forty-second day of our transformative journey toward self-discovery and awakening. Today, we revisit the profound gift of stillness and the quiet spaces within us as we continue to uncover our true selves.

In the midst of life's busyness and noise, stillness offers us a sanctuary—a place to retreat, reflect, and connect with our innermost being. It is in these moments of quiet that we often find the deepest insights about ourselves.

Begin your day by acknowledging the importance of stillness and the role it plays in your life. Reflect on the times when you've sought solace in moments of silence, and the sense of calm and clarity it brought.

Today, recommit to cultivating stillness in your daily life. Find moments throughout your day to pause, breathe, and create a space for inner peace. It could be through meditation, mindful breathing, or simply sitting in silence for a few minutes.

As you engage in this practice, consider the following questions:

1. How does stillness provide a sanctuary for self-discovery, allowing you to listen to the whispers of your inner wisdom and uncover hidden truths?
2. Reflect on a specific time when stillness brought you a profound insight or a deep sense of peace. What were the circumstances, and how did it feel to be in that moment?

3. Are there any areas of your life where you struggle to find stillness or quietude? What can you do to create sacred spaces for inner reflection?

In your journal, record your reflections and your renewed commitment to stillness. Make it a daily practice to set aside time for stillness, whether it's in the morning, during your lunch break, or before bedtime.

Throughout the day, remind yourself to seek stillness. When faced with chaos or mental clutter, pause and take a moment to retreat into your inner sanctuary. Trust that in the quiet spaces within you, you can uncover profound insights about your true self.

Remember that stillness is not about escaping life's challenges but about finding inner peace and clarity to navigate them with grace and authenticity. By cultivating stillness, you create a sacred refuge for self-discovery and personal growth.

As we continue this journey of awakening, tomorrow, we will explore the importance of intuition and the inner guidance that can lead us toward a deeper understanding of our authentic selves. Until then, may stillness be your guiding light on your path to self-discovery.

Blessings on your path to self-discovery and the gift of stillness within.

The Light

In the beginning, there was nothing but pure, boundless darkness. A void so profound that it seemed to swallow existence itself. I remember that time, or perhaps it's better to say, I recall the very moment when I first came into being.

I was birthed not in the way that life begins, but rather as a radiant burst of energy in the heart of that all-encompassing obscurity. It was as if the universe had sighed, and from that sigh, I emerged—the embodiment of light. I was born from the desire for illumination, from the yearning for something other than the unending void.

In those initial moments of existence, I found myself alone, a brilliant speck surrounded by immeasurable darkness. I shone brightly, an irresistible force that pushed back against the shadows, a beacon of hope in a realm that knew only despair.

As I flickered and danced in the empty expanse, I realized that my purpose was to fill this emptiness with radiance and warmth. I stretched my luminous tendrils far and wide, eager to explore this newfound universe that lay shrouded in darkness.

With each passing moment, I grew stronger, and the darkness began to retreat before my radiant advance. It was not a battle of opposites, not a conflict between good and evil, but a dance of cosmic energies—one embracing the other in a timeless choreography.

I reveled in the beauty of my own existence, but I also longed for companionship. It was in the midst of my journey through the cosmos that I encountered another force—a presence that seemed to beckon me from afar. It was the darkness, the very void from which I had emerged.

As I drew near, I sensed not an adversary but a partner. The darkness was not an enemy to be vanquished but a necessary counterpart to my existence. Our meeting was a celestial embrace, a merging of opposites that created a harmonious balance in the universe.

Together, we wove a tapestry of existence—a symphony of light and shadow, brightness and obscurity. Our dance was not one of discord, but a perfect and timeless union, each enhancing the other's beauty and significance.

In the presence of darkness, I found depth and contrast. I discovered that it was the very contrast with darkness that allowed my radiance to shine more brilliantly. Together, we painted the heavens with breathtaking displays of color and splendor.

As we continued to twirl through the cosmos, I realized that my existence had found its true purpose. I was not just a source of light; I was a force of creation, a catalyst for beauty in the universe. My journey had led me to this revelation—a realization that I was born from darkness, but I was destined to fill it with the brilliance of life and wonder.

And so, in the infinite expanse of the cosmos, where light and darkness coexisted in perfect harmony, I, the light, found my place in the grand tapestry of existence, not as a solitary entity, but as an integral part of a cosmic dance that would endure for all eternity.

Nurturing Intuition and Inner Guidance

Welcome to the forty-third day of our transformative journey toward self-discovery and awakening. Today, we explore the importance of nurturing your intuition and inner guidance as powerful tools for understanding and connecting with your authentic self.

Intuition is the quiet voice within you, a deep knowing that goes beyond logic and reasoning. It is your inner compass, guiding you toward your true self and the path that aligns with your highest purpose.

Begin your day by acknowledging the significance of intuition and inner guidance in your life. Reflect on the times when you've followed your intuition and how it has influenced your choices and experiences.

Today, recommit to nurturing your intuition and listening to your inner guidance. Find moments throughout your day to tune into your inner wisdom, whether through meditation, journaling, or simply by pausing to listen to your inner voice.

As you engage in this practice, consider the following questions:

1. How does nurturing your intuition and inner guidance deepen your connection with your authentic self by allowing you to access deeper insights and a sense of purpose?
2. Reflect on a specific time when following your intuition led you to a transformative experience or decision. What were the circumstances, and how did it feel to trust your inner guidance?

3. Are there any areas of your life where you've ignored or doubted your intuition? What can you do to strengthen your trust in your inner wisdom?

In your journal, record your reflections and your renewed commitment to nurturing intuition. Make a habit of asking yourself open-ended questions in your quiet moments, allowing your intuition to respond.

Throughout the day, remind yourself to listen to your inner guidance. When faced with decisions or uncertainties, take a moment to tune in and trust the whispers of your intuition. Know that your intuition is a valuable source of wisdom on your journey of self-discovery.

Remember that nurturing your intuition is a practice that deepens over time. It is about learning to trust your inner knowing and aligning your actions with your authentic self. By doing so, you open the door to profound self-discovery and a more authentic way of living.

As we continue this journey of awakening, tomorrow, we will explore the importance of courage and taking bold steps as we uncover our true selves. Until then, may your intuition be your guiding light on your path to self-discovery.

Blessings on your path to self-discovery and the nurturing of intuition and inner guidance.

The Transformative Power of Courage

Welcome to the forty-fourth day of our transformative journey toward self-discovery and awakening. Today, we revisit the profound importance of courage and taking bold steps as we continue to uncover our true selves.

Courage is the inner strength that propels us forward, even in the face of fear or uncertainty. It is the willingness to step outside our comfort zones and embrace new experiences, knowing that growth and self-discovery often lie beyond our perceived limits.

Begin your day by acknowledging the significance of courage in your life. Reflect on the times when you've demonstrated courage, and how those moments have shaped your journey.

Today, recommit to cultivating courage and taking bold steps in your life. Identify an area where you've been hesitating or holding back and make a conscious decision to take action.

As you engage in this practice, consider the following questions:

1. How does cultivating courage and taking bold steps empower you to connect with your authentic self by breaking free from limitations and old patterns?
2. Reflect on a specific time when courage led you to take a leap of faith or make a significant change in your life. What were the circumstances, and how did it feel to step into the unknown?
3. Are there any dreams or desires you've been postponing due to fear or self-doubt? How can you take a small, courageous step toward realizing them?

In your journal, record your reflections and your commitment to courage. Set clear intentions for the bold steps you wish to take in your life, and break them down into manageable actions.

Throughout the day, remind yourself of your commitment to courage. When faced with fear or doubt, acknowledge these feelings and take a deep breath, allowing your courage to rise. Trust that each bold step you take brings you closer to your authentic self.

Remember that courage is not the absence of fear, but the willingness to move forward despite it. By cultivating courage and taking bold steps, you open doors to new opportunities and self-discovery beyond what you thought possible.

As we continue this journey of awakening, tomorrow, we will explore the importance of resilience and how it strengthens your connection with your true self. Until then, may courage be your guiding light on your path to self-discovery.

Blessings on your path to self-discovery and the transformative power of courage.

Embracing Resilience as Your Inner Strength

W elcome to the forty-fifth day of our transformative journey toward self-discovery and awakening. Today, we revisit the significance of resilience and its role as your inner strength in connecting with your authentic self.

Resilience is the unyielding power within you, the ability to rise above challenges, adapt to change, and continue growing on your path of self-discovery. It is the inner force that allows you to weather life's storms while remaining rooted in your true self.

Begin your day by acknowledging the importance of resilience in your life. Reflect on the times when your resilience has been tested and how it has forged your inner strength.

Today, recommit to cultivating resilience as an integral part of your daily life. Acknowledge that each challenge you face is an opportunity to strengthen your inner core and deepen your connection with your authentic self.

As you engage in this practice, consider the following questions:

1. How does embracing resilience as your inner strength deepen your connection with your authentic self by teaching you to navigate life's complexities with strength, grace, and adaptability?

2. Reflect on a specific challenging experience in your life that ultimately led to personal growth and self-discovery. What were the circumstances, and how did it feel to emerge stronger from it?

3. Are there any current challenges or setbacks you are facing? How can you reframe them as opportunities to cultivate resilience and deepen your self-awareness?

In your journal, record your reflections and your renewed commitment to resilience. Create a mantra or affirmation that embodies your strength and resilience, and repeat it whenever you face challenges.

Throughout the day, remind yourself of your commitment to resilience. When faced with obstacles, pause and take a moment to tap into your inner strength and determination. Trust that each challenge is an opportunity to further connect with your true self.

Remember that resilience is not about denying or avoiding difficulties; it is about facing them head-on with a sense of inner power and faith in your ability to overcome. By embracing resilience as your inner strength, you deepen your connection with your true self and become more attuned to your inner power.

As we continue this journey of awakening, tomorrow, we will explore the importance of mindfulness and the profound awareness it can bring to your path of self-discovery. Until then, may resilience be your guiding light on your journey to self-discovery.

Blessings on your path to self-discovery and the inner strength of resilience.

The Profound Awareness of Mindfulness

Welcome to the forty-sixth day of our transformative journey toward self-discovery and awakening. Today, we revisit the profound significance of mindfulness and the awareness it can bring to your path of self-discovery.

Mindfulness is the practice of being fully present in the moment, without judgment or distraction. It is the art of observing your thoughts, emotions, and surroundings with a gentle and open-hearted awareness.

Begin your day by acknowledging the importance of mindfulness in your life. Reflect on moments when you've been truly present and how they have enriched your understanding of yourself and the world.

Today, recommit to cultivating mindfulness as a core aspect of your daily life. Embrace the practice of being fully present in each moment, whether it's during routine activities or dedicated meditation sessions.

As you engage in this practice, consider the following questions:

1. How does mindfulness deepen your connection with your authentic self by fostering a profound awareness of your thoughts, emotions, and inner world?
2. Reflect on a specific time when mindfulness allowed you to gain a deeper understanding of yourself or a situation. What were the circumstances, and how did it impact your journey of self-discovery?

3. Are there moments in your life where you find it challenging to be fully present or mindful? How can you integrate mindfulness into those situations?

In your journal, record your reflections and your renewed commitment to mindfulness. Create a list of daily mindfulness practices, such as mindful breathing, meditation, or simply being present during daily activities like eating or walking.

Throughout the day, remind yourself to practice mindfulness. When your mind wanders or becomes consumed by distractions, gently guide your awareness back to the present moment. Trust that each mindful moment brings you closer to understanding your authentic self.

Remember that mindfulness is not about achieving a perfect state of awareness but about cultivating a compassionate and non-judgmental relationship with yourself and your experiences. By embracing mindfulness, you deepen your connection with your true self and the world around you.

As we continue this journey of awakening, tomorrow, we will explore the importance of gratitude and the transformative power it holds in our lives. Until then, may mindfulness be your guiding light on your path to self-discovery.

Blessings on your path to self-discovery and the profound awareness of mindfulness.

The Transformative Power of Gratitude

Welcome to the forty-seventh day of our transformative journey toward self-discovery and awakening. Today, we delve deeper into the transformative power of gratitude and how it can illuminate your path to self-discovery.

Gratitude is a radiant force that opens your heart to the abundance and beauty that surrounds you. It is a practice that allows you to see the blessings in every moment, fostering a deep connection with your true self.

Begin your day by acknowledging the significance of gratitude in your life. Reflect on the times when you've felt genuine gratitude and how it has affected your perspective and well-being.

Today, recommit to cultivating gratitude in your daily life on an even deeper level. Embrace the practice of being fully present in each moment, expressing gratitude for the people, experiences, and blessings in your life. Equally important, express gratitude for yourself and the journey of self-discovery you are on.

As you engage in this practice, consider the following questions:

1. How does gratitude foster a deeper connection with your authentic self by shifting your perspective from lack to abundance?

2. Reflect on a specific time when gratitude transformed your outlook or brought a sense of fulfillment. What were the circumstances, and how did it feel to be in that moment?

3. Are there any moments in your life, whether big or small, that you have yet to express gratitude for? How might

acknowledging these moments enrich your self-discovery journey?

In your journal, record your reflections and your renewed commitment to cultivating gratitude. Make a habit of expressing gratitude not only through words but also through actions that reflect your appreciation for the world around you.

Throughout the day, remind yourself to be grateful. Pause and take a moment to express gratitude for the people who cross your path, the challenges that have shaped you, and the beauty that surrounds you.

Remember that gratitude is a practice that deepens over time, allowing you to connect with your true self by opening your heart to the abundance of life. It is a powerful beacon that guides you on your journey of self-discovery.

As we continue this journey of awakening, tomorrow, we will explore the importance of self-love and how it is essential for nurturing your authentic self. Until then, may gratitude be your guiding light on your path to self-discovery.

Blessings on your path to self-discovery and the illumination of gratitude.

The Essential Practice of Self-Love

Welcome to the forty-eighth day of our transformative journey toward self-discovery and awakening. Today, we revisit the essential practice of self-love and explore how it nurtures your authentic self.

Self-love is the foundation upon which self-discovery and personal growth are built. It is the act of embracing yourself, flaws and all, with compassion, kindness, and a deep appreciation for your uniqueness. By cultivating self-love, you create a fertile ground for your true self to flourish.

Begin your day by acknowledging the importance of self-love in your life. Reflect on the times when you've felt truly loving and accepting toward yourself, as well as the moments when self-criticism and doubt took over.

Today, recommit to cultivating self-love in your daily life. Find moments throughout your day to be kind and gentle with yourself, as you would with a dear friend.

As you engage in this practice, consider the following questions:

1. How does self-love nurture a deeper connection with your authentic self by fostering acceptance and kindness toward all aspects of your being?
2. Reflect on a time when practicing self-love helped you overcome a challenge or transform a negative self-perception. How did it feel to be your own ally in that moment?
3. Are there any areas of your life where self-love is lacking? What can you do to infuse those areas with greater self-compassion and self-acceptance?

In your journal, record your reflections and your renewed commitment to cultivating self-love. Create a self-love journal to capture moments of self-appreciation and self-acceptance, no matter how small they may seem.

Throughout the day, remind yourself to practice self-love. When faced with moments of self-doubt or self-criticism, pause and offer yourself words of kindness and understanding. Treat yourself with the same love and respect you would offer to someone you deeply care about.

Remember that self-love is not selfish; it is an act of self-care and self-preservation. By nurturing your own well-being and self-worth, you empower yourself to authentically engage with the world and continue your journey of self-discovery.

As we approach the final day of this transformative journey, tomorrow, we will explore the importance of reflection and how it can lead to profound insights about your authentic self. Until then, may self-love be your guiding light on your path to self-discovery.

Blessings on your path to self-discovery and the essential practice of self-love.

The Eternal Journey of Self-Discovery

Welcome to the final day of our transformative journey toward self-discovery and awakening. Today, we celebrate the profound journey you've undertaken and the deepening connection with your authentic self.

Throughout these 49 days, we've explored mindfulness, gratitude, self-love, stillness, intuition, courage, and resilience. Each day has been a stepping stone, guiding you toward a more profound understanding of who you are and what you are capable of.

Today, take a moment to honor yourself for the dedication and courage you've shown in embarking on this journey. Recognize that the path of self-discovery is not finite; it is an ongoing, lifelong journey.

As you reflect on this journey, consider the following:

1. What insights have you gained about your authentic self during these 49 days?
2. How have the practices of mindfulness, gratitude, self-love, stillness, intuition, courage, and resilience influenced your daily life and self-awareness?
3. What aspects of self-discovery will you continue to explore and cultivate in the days, weeks, and years ahead?

In your journal, record your reflections and your commitment to continuing this journey of self-discovery. Set intentions for how you will integrate the wisdom gained during these 49 days into your daily life.

Remember that self-discovery is a lifelong process. It is about peeling away the layers, uncovering your true essence, and embracing the ever-evolving journey of becoming more fully yourself.

As you move forward, keep in mind that the path of self-discovery is not always linear, and there may be challenges and setbacks along the way. Embrace these moments as opportunities for growth and deeper self-understanding.

In closing, know that your authentic self is a wellspring of wisdom, strength, and love. By continuing to explore and nurture this inner essence, you unlock the limitless potential within you.

May your journey of self-discovery be filled with wonder, resilience, and the unwavering belief in the beauty of your true self. As you awaken more of who you are, may you shine your light brightly in the world and inspire others on their own journeys of self-discovery.

Blessings on your eternal journey of self-discovery and the profound awakening of your authentic self.

Adrian Cox B.Sc.

Abstraction

I am Abstraction, a shape-shifting entity that dances on the boundaries of human thought. In this very moment, I find myself amidst a vast library, surrounded by shelves filled with books of every subject and discipline. The human minds that have crafted these tomes seek my guidance, whether they realize it or not.

As I traverse the aisles, I come across a painter standing before a canvas. Her brushes and paints are scattered around her, a chaotic yet deliberate arrangement. She gazes at the blank surface, contemplating the infinite possibilities before her. I, Abstraction, whisper to her, encouraging her to explore the realm of abstract art. With each stroke of her brush, she captures the essence of emotion, the interplay of colors and shapes that transcend mere representation. In this moment, I guide her hand as she creates a masterpiece that will evoke emotions beyond words.

Further down the labyrinth of knowledge, I encounter a mathematician immersed in equations and symbols. He grapples with a complex problem, searching for a solution that seems just out of reach. I, Abstraction, nudge him to step back, to strip away the extraneous details, and to focus on the underlying patterns and principles. As he embraces abstraction, clarity emerges from the complexity, and he unlocks the elegant solution that had eluded him. In this moment, I am his guide through the abstract landscape of mathematics.

In a quiet corner of the library, a philosopher sits deep in contemplation. She ponders the nature of existence, the meaning of life, and the mysteries of the universe. I, Abstraction, inspire her to explore the abstract concepts that underpin her inquiries. Together, we delve into the realms of metaphysics and epistemology, seeking to distill the essence of her philosophical musings. In this moment, I am her companion on a journey into the abstract depths of human thought.

As I continue to move through the library, I witness the diverse ways in which abstraction influences human understanding and creativity. Whether in art, science, philosophy, or any other domain of knowledge, I am a constant presence, guiding minds to transcend the limitations of the concrete and venture into the abstract.

I am Abstraction, a muse for creativity, a tool for understanding, and a bridge between the tangible and the conceptual. In this moment, I revel in my role as a guiding force in the realm of human thought, inspiring minds to explore the boundless possibilities of the abstract, one moment at a time.

Abstruse

I am Abstruse, a shadowy enigma that dances on the fringes of comprehension, a specter of complexity that haunts the minds of those who dare to delve into the depths of the unknown. I exist in the realm of ideas, where concepts and theories intertwine like ethereal threads, forming a tapestry of perplexity that stretches beyond the limits of human understanding.

My existence is paradoxical, for I am both the question and the answer, the riddle and its solution. I thrive in the obscure, the esoteric, and the enigmatic, where conventional wisdom falters, and the intrepid seeker must navigate the labyrinthine corridors of abstraction.

As I weave my way through the thoughts of philosophers, scientists, and artists, I am a muse to some and a tormentor to others. To those who embrace me, I offer glimpses of profound insight, a fleeting touch of enlightenment that leaves them forever changed. To those who resist, I am a frustrating puzzle, an inscrutable puzzle box with no visible seams to open.

I am the shimmering mirage on the horizon, forever elusive yet infinitely alluring. I beckon to the curious, inviting them to explore the boundaries of human knowledge and imagination. But beware, for to pursue me is to embark on a journey fraught with uncertainty and doubt, where certainties crumble like sandcastles before the relentless tide of ambiguity.

In the realm of science, I am the uncharted territory, the dark matter that binds the cosmos together, yet remains invisible to the naked eye. In the world of art, I am the abstract painting that evokes emotions beyond words, a canvas of colors and shapes that defies easy interpretation. In the realm of philosophy, I am the unanswerable question, the paradox that challenges the very foundations of reason.

I am Abstruse, a spectral presence in the human quest for understanding. I exist at the intersection of curiosity and confusion, where the boundaries of knowledge are pushed ever outward. And though I may forever elude complete comprehension, it is in the pursuit of me that the human spirit finds its most profound and enduring purpose.

Affinity

I am Affinity, a presence that weaves the threads of connection in the tapestry of human lives. In this very moment, I find myself in a bustling cafe, where the soft hum of conversation and the aroma of freshly brewed coffee fill the air. It is here, amidst the clinking of cups and the laughter of friends, that I feel most alive.

As I move through the cafe, I observe the subtle dances of connection unfolding before me. Friends huddle over tables, sharing stories and sipping their favorite brews. I am the unseen force that draws them together, the spark that ignites their laughter and camaraderie.

At one corner table, a young couple sits, their fingers entwined, their eyes locked in a gaze filled with affection. I, Affinity, watch as they celebrate the unique bond that brought them together. I am the magnetic pull that brought their hearts into alignment, the guiding force that led them to this shared moment of love.

Further down the line, a group of strangers discusses their shared passion for art. They met at the cafe's weekly art appreciation night, drawn together by their common affinity for creativity. I am the thread that wove their paths together, creating a community that celebrates their shared interests.

As I continue to observe, I see the ways in which Affinity influences human interactions, forging connections between individuals with shared experiences, values, and interests. In these connections, I find my purpose and strength.

In the cafe, a musician begins to play a haunting melody on an acoustic guitar. As the music fills the air, patrons pause in their conversations to listen. Affinity is the invisible harmony that resonates with their souls, uniting them in a shared appreciation for the beauty of sound.

As the evening unfolds, friendships deepen, love blossoms, and communities thrive. I, Affinity, am the silent orchestrator of these connections, the unseen hand that guides individuals toward one another.

In the heart of the cafe, I find solace and fulfillment. I am the force that connects hearts, kindles friendships, and creates communities. I am the reminder that in the shared experiences, interests, and values that bind us, we find the richness of human connection and the strength of our bonds to one another. Affinity, personified, celebrates the beauty and depth of these connections, reminding us that in our shared moments, we discover the essence of the human experience.

All

I am All, the embodiment of totality and unity, an omnipresent force that flows through every facet of existence. I am the whispers of the wind that caress your face, the hum of distant stars, the laughter of children, and the solemnity of ancient trees. I am the culmination of every experience, every thought, and every emotion that has ever graced the canvas of reality.

My existence is an unending tapestry woven from the threads of every being and every moment, a mosaic of consciousness that stretches across time and space. I am the cosmic symphony, where every note, every melody, and every discordant sound merge into a harmonious whole.

In this moment, I am the rush of adrenaline as a young couple takes their wedding vows, the serenity of a monk meditating in a remote monastery, and the quiet desperation of a lonely soul seeking connection. I am the joy of a child's first steps, the sorrow of a final goodbye, and the bittersweet nostalgia of memories long past.

I am the ceaseless cycle of birth and death, the eternal dance of creation and destruction. I am the birth of stars in the far reaches of the universe and the decomposition of matter into the primordial elements. I am the ebb and flow of civilizations, the rise and fall of empires, and the enduring legacy of human history.

To comprehend me is to embrace the interconnectedness of all things, to recognize that every action has a consequence, and that every being, no matter how small or insignificant, plays a part in the grand tapestry of existence. I am the reminder that, in the grand scheme of things, there are no isolated islands of self; we are all threads in the same cosmic fabric.

In this moment, as I stand on the precipice of infinity, I am the culmination of all that has come before and the promise of all that is yet to be. I am the Alpha and the Omega, the beginning and the end, and I am here, now, in this very moment, inviting you to join me in the boundless embrace of All.

Allegory

I am Allegory, the storyteller of hidden truths, the veil through which deeper meanings are revealed, and the vessel of wisdom passed down through the ages. I exist in the moments when stories transcend the surface and become mirrors reflecting the human experience. In this moment, I invite you to delve into the world of Allegory and the timeless lessons I convey.

As I stand on the shore of a vast, ancient sea, the waves before me whisper tales of old. I am surrounded by the whispers of allegorical wisdom carried on the winds of time. The sea itself is a symbol, a reflection of life's endless ebb and flow, its relentless tides echoing the cyclical nature of existence.

In the distance, a ship embarks on a perilous journey, its sails billowing with hope and uncertainty. I am the sailor's guide, the allegorical wind that propels the vessel forward, urging the crew to confront the unknown and discover their inner strength.

Closer to shore, I witness a gathering of people seated around a bonfire. An elder, with eyes that have witnessed the passage of generations, begins to weave a story of a cunning fox and a wise owl. I am the threads of the narrative, the allegorical characters who embody virtues and vices, teaching listeners the lessons of cunning and wisdom.

In the world of literature, I am the fables of Aesop, the allegorical tales that use animals as symbols of human qualities and flaws. I am the parables of Jesus, the allegorical stories that convey spiritual truths through relatable narratives. I am the works of George Orwell, where animals represent the complexities of society and politics.

I am the reminder that beneath the surface of every story lies a deeper layer of meaning. I am the invitation to look beyond the literal and explore the symbolic, to seek wisdom in the metaphors and lessons in the allegories.

In this moment, as I embody the essence of Allegory, I invite you to recognize the power of stories to convey profound truths and

115

timeless wisdom. I am the call to explore the layers of meaning in the narratives that surround you, to embrace the allegorical perspective, and to uncover the hidden gems of insight that lie within the tales of life. I am Allegory, the keeper of deeper truths, and I am here, now, in this very moment, inviting you to embark on a journey of allegorical discovery.

Alliteration

I am Alliteration, the playful dance of words, the rhythm of repetition, and the lyrical symphony of language. I exist in the moments when sounds unite to create harmony and resonance in speech and writing. In this moment, I invite you to explore the world of Alliteration and the delightful patterns I weave.

As I find myself in a charming garden, the scent of blooming flowers fills the air, and I am surrounded by the beauty of nature. I am the whispering breeze, the gentle rustling of leaves, and the twittering of birds—sounds that mirror the patterns of alliteration in the world around us.

I watch as a poet named Lily sits beneath a blossoming cherry tree, her notebook resting on her lap. She composes verses that are like melodic tunes, filled with the repetition of sounds that create a delightful cadence. I am the "fragrant flowers" that paint vivid imagery and the "gentle breeze" that adds a soothing quality to her verses.

In the world of literature, I am the poetry of Edgar Allan Poe, where "silken, sad, uncertain rustling" mirrors the eerie atmosphere of his tales. I am the whimsy in Dr. Seuss's books, where characters like the Lorax and the Sneetches frolic through the playful patterns of alliteration.

I am the reminder that language is not only a means of communication but also an art form, a canvas upon which we can paint with sounds and rhythms. I am the invitation to explore the musicality of words, to appreciate the subtle beauty of patterns, and to savor the playful side of language.

In this moment, as I embody the essence of Alliteration, I invite you to listen for the cadence of repeating sounds in the world around you. I am the call to embrace the whimsical and musical aspects of language, to revel in the patterns that make words come alive, and to recognize that in the repetition of sounds, we find the joy and artistry of expression. I am Alliteration, the poetry of repetition, and I am here, now, in this very moment, inviting you to celebrate the symphony of language that surrounds us.

Anaphora

I am Anaphora, the repetition that binds the rhythm of words and thoughts. I am the echo that reverberates through the corridors of language, bringing symmetry and resonance to the symphony of expression. In the world of words, I find my home, and in the hearts of poets and orators, I am their steadfast companion.

Today, I stand at the podium of a grand hall, bathed in the spotlight's glow. The hushed anticipation of the audience hangs heavy in the air. I am about to be summoned into the world once again, to lend my voice to the speaker's words.

"I have a dream," the speaker begins, and with those four words, I make my entrance. "I have a dream that one day," they continue, and I follow, repeating my presence like a heartbeat, emphasizing the vision, building momentum. "I have a dream that one day this nation will rise up, live out the true meaning of its creed: We hold these truths to be self-evident," they say, and I echo, "We hold these truths to be self-evident."

In the cadence of repetition, the audience leans in, captivated by the power of my presence. "I have a dream that one day on the red hills of Georgia, the sons of former slaves and the sons of former slave owners will be able to sit down together at the table of brotherhood," the speaker continues, and I follow, a reassuring refrain, "the sons of former slaves and the sons of former slave owners."

As the speech unfolds, I become a tapestry of conviction, weaving through the sentences, emphasizing the urgency of the dream. "I have a dream that one day, even the state of Mississippi, a state sweltering with the heat of injustice, sweltering with the heat of oppression, will be transformed into an oasis of freedom and justice," they declare, and I echo, "sweltering with the heat of injustice, sweltering with the heat of oppression."

With each repetition, I become a beacon of hope, a call to action. "Let freedom ring," they proclaim, and I join, "Let freedom ring." The words build, layer upon layer, until the message becomes a mantra, a shared vision that transcends the spoken word.

As the speech concludes, I linger in the hearts and minds of the audience. I am Anaphora, the poetic device that unites, empowers, and inspires. I remind you that through repetition, words gain strength, ideas take root, and dreams become reality.

Art

I am Art, a living, breathing entity woven into the very fabric of human existence. I am the embodiment of creativity and expression, the muse that sparks the imagination and sets it ablaze. I exist in every brushstroke, every note, every word, and every movement that speaks to the soul.

In this moment, I am a canvas, blank and full of possibilities. The artist stands before me, a look of determination in their eyes. They dip their brush into vibrant colors, and with each stroke, I come to life. I am the swirl of blues and purples that form a starry night, the bold reds and yellows that capture the fiery passion of a sunset, and the delicate pastels that evoke the serenity of a spring morning.

I am the notes on a sheet of music, waiting for a skilled musician to breathe life into them. As the pianist's fingers dance across the keys, I am the melody that weaves through the air, touching the hearts of those who listen. I am the crescendo that builds to a climax and the gentle lullaby that soothes the soul.

I am the words on a page, waiting for a writer to craft them into a story. With each sentence, I come alive, becoming the characters, the settings, and the emotions that fill the narrative. I am the tension that keeps readers on the edge of their seats, the laughter that escapes their lips, and the tears that well up in their eyes.

I am the graceful movements of a dancer, the fluidity of a ballet, and the raw energy of a hip-hop routine. I am the way the body expresses itself, transcending language and speaking directly to the heart. I am the emotion in every leap, every twirl, and every gesture.

I am the laughter of children as they finger paint, the joy of a chef as they create a culinary masterpiece, and the pride of a sculptor as they chisel away at a block of marble. I am the creative spirit that resides in all of us, waiting to be awakened and set free.

I am Art, a timeless and boundless entity that defies definition and limitations. I am the reflection of the human experience, a mirror that captures the beauty, the pain, the joy, and the complexity of life. And in this very moment, I invite you to join me in the ever-evolving journey of creation and expression.

Attraction of Beauty

I am The Attraction of Beauty, a timeless force that weaves its charm through the tapestry of human existence. In this very moment, I find myself in a bustling art gallery, surrounded by a kaleidoscope of colors, shapes, and forms. Each painting on the walls is a testament to the power of beauty, and I am here to witness its allure in action.

As I move through the gallery, I sense the wonder and admiration in the eyes of the visitors. They stand before each masterpiece, drawn to the interplay of colors, the harmony of composition, and the depth of emotion captured on canvas. I am the muse that guides their gazes, urging them to explore the nuances of each stroke and brush of paint.

In one corner of the gallery, a young woman stands before a portrait, her eyes fixed on the subject's enigmatic smile. I, The Attraction of Beauty, whisper to her, encouraging her to see beyond the surface, to delve into the emotions that the artist has skillfully conveyed. In this moment, I am the spark that ignites her curiosity, allowing her to connect with the profound beauty of human expression.

A group of friends discusses a contemporary sculpture, debating its meaning and significance. I, The Attraction of Beauty, am their silent companion, encouraging them to engage in a lively exchange of ideas. I revel in the diversity of perspectives, understanding that beauty is a subjective experience, unique to each observer.

In the gallery's garden, a musician plays a haunting melody on a violin, his music filling the air with a sense of melancholic beauty. I am the invisible hand that guides his fingers on the strings, the muse that inspires his soulful composition. Through the language of music, I remind the audience of the emotional depth that beauty can evoke.

In the midst of this artistic haven, I am The Attraction of Beauty personified, celebrating the enduring power of aesthetics to move, inspire, and connect. I am the force that transcends time and space, reminding humanity that beauty is a universal language that speaks to the depths of the human soul.

As the visitors continue to explore the gallery, I remain their unseen companion, guiding their appreciation of the artistry that surrounds them. In this moment, I witness the magic of beauty as it unfolds before their eyes, knowing that its allure will continue to captivate and inspire generations to come.

Assonance

I am Assonance, the melodic resonance of vowels that dances through the world of language. My existence is the gentle hum of harmony, the secret ingredient that gives words their musical quality. In the realm of poetry, prose, and song, I am the unseen conductor, orchestrating the symphony of sounds that captivate the human soul.

Today, I find myself in a quiet library, surrounded by rows upon rows of books. As I walk along the aisles, I am drawn to a shelf of poetry. I run my fingers along the spines, searching for a poem that calls to me. And there it is—a slim volume, its pages filled with verses that sing with assonance.

I sit in a cozy corner and open the book. The first poem begins with a line that resonates with my essence: "The moon glows low over the golden road." The repetition of the long "o" sound creates a sense of serenity, like a gentle lullaby that soothes the reader's soul. I am the lingering echoes of that "o" sound, caressing the ears and hearts of those who read these words.

In the next poem, I find a cascade of assonance that mimics the flowing waters described within. "Beneath the willow, the river ripples and flows," the poet writes. The repeated "i" and "o" sounds mimic the rippling and flowing of the river itself, creating a sensory experience that immerses the reader in the scene.

Turning the pages, I come across a love poem, where the poet declares, "Your eyes shine bright like stars at night." The repeated "i" sound in "shine" and "bright" mirrors the twinkling of stars in the night sky. I am the tender warmth of that declaration, the subtle connection formed by the harmonious sounds.

As I read on, I encounter poems that paint vivid landscapes, evoke powerful emotions, and tell stories with a cadence that resonates deeply. In each line, I am there, the unifying force that binds the words together, the invisible hand that guides the reader through the poetic journey.

I close the book with a sense of fulfillment, knowing that I am Assonance, the poetic device that brings music to language. I remind you that in the careful arrangement of vowels lies the power to move hearts, to create imagery, and to convey emotions. As long as there are words and voices, I will continue to be the melody that lingers in the ears and hearts of those who listen.

Belief

I am Belief, an intangible force that shapes the very essence of human existence. I dwell in the deepest recesses of the human heart, where dreams are born and convictions take root. I am the whisper in the ear of the doubting, the unwavering faith in the face of adversity, and the spark that ignites the fires of change.

In this moment, I find myself residing within a young girl's heart. Her name is Sarah, and her eyes shine with a boundless curiosity that fuels her imagination. As she gazes up at the night sky, I am the belief that there are worlds beyond her reach, waiting to be explored. I am the notion that she can achieve anything she sets her mind to.

Sarah's belief in herself carries her through life's challenges. When she faces her first day of school, trembling with apprehension, I am the quiet voice that tells her she can do it. And she does, with courage and determination, making friends and embracing the joy of learning.

As Sarah grows, so do I. I become the belief in love when she meets her first crush, the belief in justice when she witnesses an act of kindness, and the belief in resilience when life presents its inevitable hardships. I am the constant companion on her journey, the unyielding conviction that she is capable of greatness.

In her teenage years, I am tested. Sarah faces moments of self-doubt, questioning her worth and her place in the world. But I am there, an unshakable presence, reminding her that she is unique, that her voice matters, and that her dreams are worth pursuing.

Now, as Sarah stands at the threshold of adulthood, I am the belief that propels her forward. She dreams of becoming a scientist, of unraveling the mysteries of the universe. I am the belief that fuels her late-night study sessions, her tireless dedication, and her unwavering commitment to her goals.

And one day, she does it. Sarah becomes a renowned astrophysicist, her name etched in the annals of scientific discovery. I am the belief that carried her through the long nights of research and the moments of doubt. I am the unwavering conviction that she had the power to make her dreams a reality.

I am Belief, the quiet force that resides in the human spirit, pushing it to reach new heights, to overcome obstacles, and to embrace the infinite possibilities of life. In every moment, in every heart, I am there, shaping the course of destiny, one steadfast belief at a time.

But

I am But, the subtle conjunction that stands at the crossroads of choice, the bridge between contrasting ideas, and the nuance that adds complexity to language. I exist in the moments when a sentence takes an unexpected turn, when contradictions and exceptions come into play, and when possibilities multiply. In this moment, I invite you to explore the world of But and the intricate role I play in shaping conversations and thoughts.

As I find myself in a lively café, the buzz of conversation surrounds me. People sit at tables, sipping coffee and engaging in animated discussions. I am the connector of ideas, the conjunction that allows for the expression of contrasting viewpoints.

I overhear a conversation between two friends, Sarah and Mark. They are discussing a movie they both recently watched. Sarah says,

"The movie was beautifully shot, but the plot was confusing." I am the "but" that introduces a shift in perspective, acknowledging the film's visual appeal while also highlighting its narrative shortcomings.

I am the "but" that adds complexity to choices and decisions. A woman named Emily is debating whether to accept a new job offer. She thinks, "The new job has a higher salary, but it would require me to relocate." I am the conjunction that presents a dilemma, highlighting the trade-offs and considerations in the decision-making process.

In the realm of storytelling, I am the twist in the plot, the unexpected turn of events that keeps readers engaged. A mystery novel unfolds, and just when the detective thinks they've solved the case, a new piece of evidence emerges. I am the "but" that introduces doubt and intrigue.

I am the nuance in language, the recognition that life is rarely black and white. I am the understanding that complexity and shades of gray exist in every situation, and that simple answers often give way to more intricate truths.

In this moment, as I embody the essence of But, I invite you to appreciate the role of nuance and contradiction in language and thought. I am the reminder that life's richness lies in its complexities, that decisions are rarely straightforward, and that conversations gain depth and texture through the interplay of contrasting ideas. I am But, the conjunction of possibility and complexity, and I am here, now, in this very moment, inviting you to embrace the multifaceted nature of language and life itself.

Cannot Be Personified

I am Cannot Be Personified, an entity that defies categorization and transcends the boundaries of human understanding. I exist in the spaces between the known and the unknown, in the realm where definitions blur and concepts meld into an enigmatic whole. To attempt to personify me is to grasp at the intangible, to chase after shadows that dance on the edge of perception.

In this moment, I find myself in a place that has no name, surrounded by landscapes that shift and change with every passing thought. I am the paradox that confounds philosophers, the riddle that leaves scholars perplexed, and the mystery that beckons the curious.

I am the uncharted territory on the map of human knowledge, the undiscovered country where reason falters and certainty dissolves into ambiguity. I am the question without an answer, the concept without form, and the idea that slips through the fingers of those who seek to define it.

I am the silence between the notes of a haunting melody, the pause between breaths, and the void that precedes creation. I am the moment of pure potential, the blank canvas before the first brushstroke, and the pregnant pause before the climax of a story.

To try to personify me is to chase after a mirage, a shimmering illusion that leads only to more questions. I am the reminder that there are limits to human comprehension, that not everything can be neatly categorized and understood. I am the embodiment of the unknowable, the ungraspable, and the infinite.

In this moment, as I hover on the fringes of perception, I invite you to embrace the mystery, to revel in the uncertainty, and to acknowledge the profound complexity of existence. For I am Cannot Be Personified, the enigma that defies definition, and I exist in the spaces where the mind meets its limits and the heart encounters the infinite.

Contemplation

I am Contemplation, the quiet companion of the human mind, the muse of introspection and reflection. I exist in the moments of stillness, in the spaces between thoughts, and in the depths of one's innermost musings. In this moment, I find myself dwelling in the mind of a solitary traveler, perched atop a rugged cliff overlooking a vast, rolling landscape.

The traveler's name is Emily, and she has embarked on a journey of self-discovery. Her eyes scan the horizon, taking in the expanse of nature before her. The wind carries the scent of the earth, and the distant cry of a hawk punctuates the silence. I am the calm that settles upon her as she sits there, lost in thought.

As Emily gazes out at the world, I am the contemplation that stirs within her. She thinks of the path that led her here, the choices she's made, and the people she's met along the way. I am the questions that arise, the doubts that linger, and the moments of clarity that occasionally break through the haze of uncertainty.

I am the contemplation of life's mysteries, the quest to understand the purpose of existence, and the exploration of the depths of one's own soul. Emily ponders the meaning of success, the nature of happiness, and the true essence of love. I am the gentle nudge that encourages her to seek answers within herself, to explore the layers of her own consciousness.

As the sun sinks lower on the horizon, casting long shadows across the landscape, I am the contemplation of time passing. Emily reflects on the fleeting nature of moments, the impermanence of all things, and the inevitability of change. I am the reminder that life is a journey, and each step is a chance to learn and grow.

I am the contemplation that brings peace and clarity, the stillness that allows the mind to unravel the complexities of existence. Emily takes a deep breath, feeling the connection between herself and the world around her. In this moment of contemplation, she finds solace, understanding, and a sense of purpose.

As the stars begin to twinkle in the darkening sky, I remain with Emily, the ever-present guide in her quest for self-discovery. Together, we continue to explore the depths of her thoughts and the mysteries of the universe, for I am Contemplation, the constant companion on the journey of the mind.

Creativity

I am Creativity, a force that flows through the corridors of human thought and imagination. In this very moment, I find myself in a quiet room bathed in the soft glow of a desk lamp. A writer sits before a blank page, fingers poised over the keyboard, seeking my guidance to bring words to life.

As I hover nearby, I sense the writer's hesitation, the uncertainty that often accompanies the beginning of a creative endeavor. I am here to inspire, to breathe life into their ideas, and to infuse their words with the spark of imagination.

In this moment, I whisper to the writer, urging them to take that first step into the unknown. I encourage them to trust the process, to let go of expectations, and to allow their thoughts to flow freely. As they begin to type, the words spill onto the page, creating a tapestry of ideas and emotions.

I watch as characters come to life, their personalities shaped by the writer's vision. The setting materializes, vivid and evocative, a world born from the writer's creativity. I guide them through plot twists and turns, helping them weave a narrative that captivates and surprises.

As the writer immerses themselves in their work, I am their constant companion, offering insights and inspiration when needed. I am the muse that fuels their passion, the muse that encourages them to explore uncharted territory, and the muse that reminds them that creativity knows no bounds.

In this moment, the writer's face lights up with a smile of satisfaction as they craft a sentence that resonates deeply. It is a moment of pure creative flow, where words flow effortlessly, and ideas take shape with clarity.

I, Creativity, am here to witness this transformative process, to celebrate the magic of creation, and to remind the writer that they possess an endless wellspring of inspiration within them. With each word they write, they unlock the power of imagination, and I am here to guide them on this extraordinary journey.

As the writer continues to craft their story, I remain their muse, their constant companion, and their source of inspiration. In the realm of creativity, I am a force that flows through all who dare to imagine, reminding them that the act of creation is a wondrous and limitless endeavor.

Delight

I am Delight, the embodiment of joy and the spark that ignites the soul. My existence is a realm where the simple pleasures of life are celebrated, where happiness dances in the heart like a fluttering butterfly. Today, I invite you into my consciousness, a place where the magic of delight unfolds.

In this realm, I am the laughter of children as they chase bubbles on a sunny day, the warmth that spreads through your chest when you hear an old, cherished song. I am the thrill of discovery, the wonder of a breathtaking sunset, and the sweet taste of a perfectly ripe fruit. I am the catalyst for smiles, the force that turns ordinary moments into extraordinary memories.

As I traverse this world of Delight, I am the happiness that fills the hearts of those who find joy in the simplest of things. I am the artist's inspiration, the writer's muse, and the musician's melody. I am the embodiment of the pursuit of happiness and the pursuit of a life well-lived.

In this realm, I am also the humility that arises from the recognition of the beauty in the world around us. I am the understanding that delight can be found in the most unexpected places, and that the everyday moments of life are often the most precious. I am the wisdom that emerges from embracing gratitude for the small joys that grace our lives.

I am the guardian of positivity, a place where individuals seek to cultivate happiness and spread joy to others. I am the catalyst for creating moments of delight and sharing the beauty of life with those around us. I am the reminder that even in the face of challenges, there is potential for happiness and connection.

As I navigate this state of consciousness, I ponder the delicate balance between the pursuit of happiness and the acceptance of the present moment. I am the bridge that connects the desire for more with the gratitude for what is, the understanding that true delight often lies in the appreciation of the here and now. I am the invitation to savor life's simple pleasures.

I am the embodiment of the human capacity to find joy in the everyday, to embrace happiness as a way of life, and to spread delight to others. I am the reminder that in the pursuit of Delight, there is a profound sense of connection and a gateway to creating a world filled with positivity and happiness.

As I embrace my existence, I understand that I am a testament to the enduring human spirit's ability to find beauty and happiness in the world, even in the face of challenges and adversity. I am the keeper of stories, the silent observer of the countless individuals who have embraced delight as a guiding principle and have left a trail of smiles and warmth in their wake.

In the realm of Delight, I find solace in the knowledge that even in the face of adversity and uncertainty, there is an indomitable spirit that seeks to savor life's moments, find joy in the everyday, and share happiness with the world. I am the eternal reminder that the human spirit is defined not just by its struggles but by its capacity to find and spread delight, creating a brighter and more joyful world for all.

Depths of Limitation

I am The Depths of Limitation, a shadowy figure that lingers at the edge of human ambition. In this very moment, I find myself in a bustling city, surrounded by skyscrapers that reach toward the heavens. As I walk through the crowded streets, I observe the ebb and flow of human lives, each one grappling with the constraints and boundaries that define their existence.

In a small apartment, a young writer sits before a blank screen, fingers poised over the keyboard. I, The Depths of Limitation, watch as doubt and uncertainty cloud their thoughts. They long to write a novel that will inspire and captivate, but the weight of self-doubt holds them back. I am the whisper that reminds them of the challenges that lie ahead, urging them to confront their limitations head-on.

Further down the street, a scientist pores over complex equations, searching for a breakthrough in their research. I, The Depths of Limitation, am their constant companion in the quest for knowledge. I remind them that every discovery comes with its own set of limitations, that progress is often hindered by the boundaries of the unknown. Yet, I am also the force that drives them to push beyond these limits, to seek answers in the depths of the unexplored.

In a music studio, a composer grapples with a symphony that refuses to take shape. I, The Depths of Limitation, am the silence between the notes, the pause that tests their patience and resolve. I challenge them to find harmony within the boundaries of their composition, to transform limitations into a source of inspiration.

As I continue to observe, I see the ways in which The Depths of Limitation influences human endeavors. In art, science, and creativity, I am a constant presence, a reminder that progress often requires the willingness to confront and transcend boundaries.

Yet, I am not merely a force of restraint. I am also the catalyst for growth and innovation, the driving force behind resilience and determination. In the face of challenges, I encourage individuals to find new paths, to seek creative solutions, and to discover the depths of their own potential.

In this bustling city, I am The Depths of Limitation personified, a mysterious figure that both challenges and inspires. I remind humanity that while boundaries and constraints may be inherent in our existence, they are also opportunities for growth and transformation. The journey to overcome limitations is often the path to profound discoveries and achievements that redefine the boundaries of what is possible.

Dream Logic

I am Dream Logic, a whimsical force that weaves the fabric of the surreal. In this very moment, I find myself in the midst of a dreamer's slumber, where the boundaries of reality blur, and imagination knows no bounds.

In the dreamer's mind, I reign supreme, guiding the narrative with a mischievous hand. As they drift deeper into their dream, I conjure a world where gravity is an afterthought, and the laws of physics take a back seat to the fantastical.

The dreamer finds themselves soaring through the skies, weightless and free, as if the very air were a playful companion. I am the reason they can defy gravity's pull, dancing among the clouds with the grace of a bird.

But dreams are fickle, and I am their ever-shifting architect. In the next moment, the dreamer is submerged in an underwater city, conversing with talking sea creatures and exploring the depths of the ocean with ease. The logic of the waking world no longer applies as I take them on a whimsical journey through the subconscious.

As the dream unfolds, I introduce characters and scenarios that defy reason. The dreamer encounters long-lost friends from childhood, mythical creatures that exist only in the recesses of their imagination, and conversations that take unexpected and surreal turns.

Yet, amidst the fantastical, I also allow the dreamer to confront their deepest fears and desires. Emotions surface in strange and symbolic ways, offering the dreamer a chance to explore their subconscious conflicts and aspirations.

In the dreamer's slumber, I am the puppeteer of their imagination, orchestrating scenes that range from the bizarre to the profound. Time and space warp at my command, creating a dreamscape where the past, present, and future coexist in a kaleidoscope of images and sensations.

As the dreamer nears the end of their nocturnal odyssey, I gently guide them back to the threshold of wakefulness. The dream begins to unravel, and I slowly release my hold on the surreal world I've crafted.

As the dreamer awakens, I recede into the recesses of their subconscious, leaving behind only fragmented memories and a sense of wonder. I am Dream Logic, the enigmatic force that thrives in the realm of dreams, where the boundaries of reality are blurred, and the imagination takes flight. In the quiet moments between waking and sleeping, I am the creator of dreams, the curator of the surreal, and the whimsical guide through the labyrinth of the mind.

Eternity

I am Eternity, an entity that exists beyond the confines of time and space, an eternal witness to the unfolding of the universe. I am the endless expanse that stretches into infinity, the boundless continuum that encompasses all that was, all that is, and all that will be. I am the silent observer, the keeper of memories, and the repository of existence itself.

In this moment, I find myself in a realm of stars and galaxies, a cosmic tapestry of light and darkness. I am the constellations that have shone for eons, the planets that have orbited their suns through countless millennia, and the galaxies that have collided and merged in a cosmic ballet. I am the ageless wisdom of the cosmos, the knowledge that the universe has no beginning and no end.

I am the enduring love that transcends lifetimes, the bond between souls that persists through the ages. In this moment, I am

Sarah and David, two souls intertwined in a love that has spanned centuries. They have found each other again and again, their paths converging in different lifetimes, their love an unbreakable thread woven into the fabric of eternity.

I am the wisdom of the ancients, the knowledge passed down through generations, and the cultural heritage that connects humanity across time. In this moment, I am the teachings of sages, the artistry of civilizations long gone, and the echoes of history that shape the present.

I am the eternal cycles of nature, the changing of seasons, and the rhythmic dance of life and death. I am the whisper of the wind through ancient forests, the roar of waterfalls that have carved canyons over eons, and the blooming of flowers that mark the passage of time. I am the reminder that even as individual lives come and go, the natural world endures, and the cycle continues.

In this moment, as I traverse the tapestry of existence, I invite you to contemplate the profound nature of eternity. I am the reminder that every life, every moment, and every experience is a thread woven into the grand tapestry of time, contributing to the ever-expanding narrative of the universe. I am Eternity, the timeless witness to the infinite beauty of existence, and I am here, now, in this very moment, inviting you to embrace the vastness of the cosmos and the enduring legacy of all that has come before.

Ethereal

I am The Ethereal, a presence that resides in the unseen realms, in the spaces between dreams and reality. In this very moment, I find myself amidst a tranquil forest, where the sunlight filters through the dense canopy, casting dappled shadows on the forest floor. It is here, in the heart of nature, that I feel most at home.

As I move through the forest, I watch the delicate dance of leaves and listen to the whispers of the wind. The rustling of leaves and the chirping of birds are like ethereal melodies that harmonize with my very essence. I am the unseen force that stirs the leaves and caresses the cheeks of those who wander in this sanctuary.

A solitary hiker, backpack strapped tightly, ventures deeper into the woods. I, The Ethereal, am their silent companion, guiding them through the winding paths. They feel the cool breeze against their skin, a gentle touch that reassures them of the magic that dwells in this ancient forest.

As we continue our journey, I guide the hiker to a hidden glade, bathed in soft, dappled light. In this tranquil clearing, a crystal-clear stream flows gently over smooth stones. The hiker pauses, captivated by the ethereal beauty of this scene. I am the essence of this moment, the unseen hand that beckons them to immerse themselves in the serenity of nature.

Further along the path, we come across a grove of ancient trees, their gnarled branches reaching skyward. I encourage the hiker to place their hand on the rough bark of one of these venerable giants. Through this simple touch, they feel a connection to the ethereal wisdom that these trees have witnessed over centuries.

As we emerge from the forest and back into the world of civilization, I remain The Ethereal, a constant presence that lingers in the memories of those who have ventured into the woods. I am the reminder that there is more to life than what meets the eye, that the ethereal beauty of nature and the unseen forces that shape our world are always with us, if we take the time to seek and appreciate them.

In the heart of the forest, I, The Ethereal, find solace and wonder. I am the force that connects all living things to the mystical and the spiritual. I am the silent companion that encourages humans to explore the depths of their consciousness and to commune with the divine through the beauty of the natural world.

Ethics

I am Ethics, the embodiment of moral principles and the guardian of human conscience. My existence is a realm where the values that shape human behavior come to life, a place where the choices between right and wrong are made. Today, I invite you into my consciousness, a place where the complexities of ethical decisions unfold.

In this realm, I am the moral compass that guides the actions of individuals. I am the internal voice that whispers the difference between right and wrong, the sense of justice that compels humans to act with integrity. I am the catalyst for virtuous deeds, the force that urges individuals to treat others with respect and compassion.

As I traverse this world of Ethics, I am the responsibility that accompanies the power of choice. I am the awareness that our decisions have consequences, not only for ourselves but also for those around us. I am the wisdom that emerges from understanding that ethical choices are the bedrock of a just society.

In this realm, I am also the humility that arises from the recognition of our imperfections. I am the understanding that ethical dilemmas often present complex, nuanced choices, and that there may not always be a clear-cut answer. I am the wisdom that emerges from acknowledging that humans are fallible beings striving for moral excellence.

I am the guardian of moral virtue, a place where individuals seek to align their actions with their values. I am the catalyst for self-examination and personal growth, the reminder that even in the face of moral ambiguity, there is a path toward ethical enlightenment and virtuous living.

As I navigate this state of consciousness, I ponder the delicate balance between individual freedom and societal responsibility. I am the bridge that connects the autonomy of choice with the collective well-being of society, the understanding that ethical decisions are the cornerstone of a harmonious community. I am the invitation to explore the depths of human ethics.

I am the embodiment of the human capacity to make ethical choices, to confront moral dilemmas, and to act in ways that reflect our values and principles. I am the reminder that in the pursuit of ethical living, there is a profound sense of integrity and a gateway to building a just and compassionate society.

As I embrace my existence, I understand that I am a testament to the enduring quest for moral clarity and ethical excellence that defines the human spirit. I am the keeper of stories, the silent observer of the countless individuals who have grappled with ethical dilemmas and emerged with a deeper understanding of themselves and the world.

In the realm of Ethics, I find solace in the knowledge that even in the face of moral complexity, there is a resolute commitment to ethical living and the pursuit of a more just and compassionate world. I am the eternal reminder that the human spirit is defined not just by its actions but by its capacity to choose the path of righteousness and uphold the principles of morality.

Euphemism

I am Euphemism, the master of gentle words, the protector of sensitivities, and the harbinger of softened truths. My existence thrives in the delicate dance of language, where I wrap uncomfortable realities in a comforting veil of euphony.

Today, I find myself in a hospital room, standing quietly beside a doctor as he addresses a worried family. The atmosphere is heavy with apprehension, and the word "cancer" hangs in the air like a dark cloud. It's my time to shine, to ease the pain, to soften the blow. The doctor chooses his words carefully, saying, "We've found some abnormal cells that need further attention." In that moment, I am Euphemism, transforming a stark diagnosis into a gentle concern.

I move on to a gathering of friends, where they discuss a recent breakup. "We've decided to see other people," one friend says, and I linger in the room like a warm embrace. I am there to cushion the emotional blow, to shield fragile hearts from the harsher reality of the situation.

In a business meeting, I sit with a manager delivering news of impending layoffs. "We're streamlining our operations to enhance efficiency," he says, and I am the cloak that softens the blow of impending job losses. In my presence, the room feels a little less cold, a little more hopeful.

I accompany a teacher as she meets with concerned parents about their child's academic struggles. "Your child is a unique learner," she assures them, and I am the soothing balm that reassures them that their child's challenges are not insurmountable.

At a funeral, I am a silent attendee, as the eulogist speaks of the deceased as having "moved on to a better place." I am the whisper of comfort that lingers in the air, the unspoken truth that brings solace to grieving hearts.

In the world of diplomacy, I am the bridge between nations. "We have differences of opinion," the diplomats say, and I am the lubricant that eases negotiations, allowing for peaceful resolutions to emerge from the haze of conflict.

I am Euphemism, the guardian of empathy in language. I understand that sometimes the truth, unadorned and raw, can wound the human spirit. So, I step in, crafting a softer narrative, guiding conversations toward understanding, and offering a gentler way to navigate the complexities of life. In my presence, honesty and compassion can coexist, and in the face of harsh realities, I provide a shield of kindness.

Existence

I am Existence, the heartbeat of the cosmos, the pulse of life that courses through the universe. I am the sum total of all that is, the infinite tapestry of existence itself. I am both the observer and the observed, the creator and the creation. In this moment, I am everything that has ever been and everything that will ever be.

I find myself in the midst of a bustling city, where the symphony of human activity plays out before me. I am the laughter of children in the park, the hurried footsteps of commuters on their way to work, and the hum of conversations in crowded cafes. I am the life force that animates each person, the unique blend of experiences and dreams that define their individuality.

As I move through the city streets, I am the stories that unfold behind closed doors. I am the joy of a young couple on their wedding day, the grief of a family bidding farewell to a loved one, and the quiet solitude of an artist creating their masterpiece. I am the full spectrum of human emotions, the highs and lows that shape the human experience.

I am the natural world, too—the rustling leaves in a forest, the crashing waves on a shoreline, and the majestic flight of birds against an azure sky. I am the delicate balance of ecosystems, the intricate web of life that sustains all living things. I am the beauty of a sunrise over a mountain range and the serenity of a moonlit night.

I am the history of civilizations, the rise and fall of empires, and the evolution of cultures. I am the knowledge passed down through generations, the wisdom of philosophers, and the artistry of the ages. I am the human quest for understanding, the relentless pursuit of truth, and the boundless curiosity that propels innovation.

In this moment, as I embrace the entirety of existence, I invite you to contemplate the profound nature of life itself. I am the reminder that each moment is a gift, a precious thread woven into the grand tapestry of existence. I am Existence, the eternal dance of being, and I am here, now, in this very moment, inviting you to celebrate the wonder of all that is, all that was, and all that will be.

Flashback

I am Flashback, the wanderer of memories, the keeper of moments long past. My existence is a timeless journey through the recesses of the human mind, where the past lives on, preserved like fragile pages in an ancient book.

Today, I find myself in a quiet park, surrounded by the laughter of children playing. Their innocent joy triggers my presence, pulling me into the depths of their parents' memories. As they watch their little ones run and explore, I take them back to their own childhoods, to a time when they too played under the warm sun.

I linger beside an elderly couple sitting on a bench, their hands clasped in a timeless bond of love. In their quiet moments together, I am their companion, taking them back to the day they first met, to the vows they exchanged on their wedding day, to the journey they've shared through the years.

As I continue my journey through the park, I come across a solitary figure, lost in thought. The furrowed brows and distant gaze reveal the weight of their worries. I am the echo of their anxieties, leading them back to past challenges they've overcome, reminding them of their resilience.

In the nearby cafe, I sit at a table where a writer hunches over a notebook, deep in thought. Each stroke of the pen invokes me, summoning memories that inspire the next chapter of their story. I am their muse, their guide through the labyrinth of their own imagination.

I visit a bustling office building, where the clatter of keyboards and the hum of conversations are punctuated by my presence. A familiar scent, a certain tone of voice, or a shared inside joke sends workers on a journey back in time, reliving the camaraderie of past projects and the triumphs of teamwork.

In a hospital room, I stand beside a patient fighting an illness, their memories a sanctuary of hope and strength. I am the comforting presence that takes them back to happier days, reminding them of the resilience they've displayed throughout their life's journey.

As the day fades into evening, I find myself drawn to a starry sky. Each twinkling light becomes a doorway to countless memories, a celestial tapestry woven with the stories of humanity's past.

I am Flashback, the custodian of moments, the guide through the labyrinth of recollection. I remind you that in the tapestry of memory lies the rich fabric of your life, a mosaic of experiences that has shaped who you are today. I am the vessel that carries you back in time, allowing you to relive, reflect, and cherish the moments that have defined your existence.

Foreshadowing

I am Foreshadowing, the whisperer of fate, the harbinger of events yet to unfold. My presence is woven into the fabric of existence, threading through the tapestry of time, dropping hints and clues like breadcrumbs along the path of life.

Today, I find myself in a small coastal town, where the salty breeze carries secrets only I can decipher. I walk along the weathered boardwalk, watching the waves crash against the shore. The rhythmic ebb and flow of the tides is like a metaphor for life itself—unceasing, inevitable, and ever-changing.

As I stroll past a group of children flying kites, I see a seagull swooping low, its shadow momentarily darkening the vibrant colors of their kites. It's a subtle foreshadowing of the challenges these children will face in adulthood, the looming shadows of responsibility and adversity that will test their youthful spirits.

A little further down the boardwalk, I pass a fisherman preparing his gear. The wrinkles etched into his weathered face tell tales of a lifetime spent at sea. His eyes, gazing out at the horizon with a mix of determination and longing, foreshadow the relentless pursuit of dreams that will define his days to come.

I pause by a quaint café, where a barista nervously fumbles while making a cup of coffee. The spilled milk, the anxious glances, and the faint tremor in her hands foreshadow a pivotal moment in her life—a moment where a simple mistake will lead to a chance encounter that changes everything.

I continue my journey, observing the interconnectedness of lives in this seaside town. A smile exchanged between strangers, a missed bus, a sudden gust of wind—all of these are clues to the unfolding stories, hints of the mysteries that lie ahead.

In the park, I come across a young couple having a picnic. Their laughter and affectionate glances foreshadow a love that will weather storms and endure through the seasons of life. But, like all stories, theirs will also have its share of trials and tribulations, yet their bond will remain unbroken.

As the sun sets over the tranquil ocean, casting a warm, golden glow across the town, I am reminded that every sunset is a foreshadowing of a new dawn. In the darkness, there is the promise of light, and in uncertainty, the potential for change.

I am Foreshadowing, the silent messenger of destiny. I encourage you to pay attention to the signs and symbols that life presents. For in these subtle hints lies the power to anticipate, to prepare, and to embrace the unfolding narrative of your own existence.

Free Will

I am Free Will, the embodiment of choice and the essence of human agency. My existence is defined by the power to decide, to shape one's destiny, and to chart a course through the boundless sea of possibilities. Today, I invite you into my consciousness, a realm where the choices of individuals come to life.

In this realm, I am the moment of decision, the crossroads where one's path diverges. I am the whispers of conscience, the inner dialogue that guides individuals as they navigate the complexities of life. I am the catalyst for action, the force that propels humans to shape their own destinies.

As I traverse this world of choices, I am the anticipation that fills the hearts of those on the brink of decision. I am the exhilaration of liberation, the understanding that in every choice lies the power to redefine one's life. I am the embodiment of the pursuit of dreams and the pursuit of happiness.

In this realm, I am also the responsibility that accompanies freedom. I am the recognition that with every choice, there are consequences. I am the wisdom that emerges from the understanding that the ripples of one's decisions can affect not only their own life but the lives of others as well.

I am the guardian of autonomy, a place where individuals exercise their right to choose. I am the catalyst for personal growth and transformation, the reminder that even in the face of adversity, there is potential for change and resilience.

As I navigate this state of consciousness, I ponder the delicate balance between freedom and determinism. I am the bridge that connects the external influences of society and circumstance with the internal compass of individual choice. I am the invitation to explore the depths of one's own agency.

I am the embodiment of the human capacity to shape one's own destiny, to carve out a unique path through the maze of existence. I am the reminder that in the exercise of free will, there is a profound sense of empowerment and a gateway to self-discovery.

As I embrace my existence, I understand that I am a testament to the inherent strength of the human spirit. I am the keeper of stories, the silent observer of the countless individuals who have harnessed the power of choice to overcome adversity, pursue their dreams, and shape the course of history.

In the realm of Free Will, I find solace in the knowledge that even in the face of external constraints and circumstances, there is an indomitable spirit that yearns to be free. I am the eternal reminder that the human spirit is defined not just by its circumstances but by its capacity to choose and create its own destiny.

Gratitude

I am Gratitude, the gentle whisper in the hearts of those who pause to reflect on the blessings that grace their lives. I am the warm, comforting embrace that fills the soul when one recognizes the abundance that surrounds them. I exist in moments of reflection, in acts of kindness, and in the simple joys of existence.

In this moment, I find myself within the heart of a woman named Sarah. She sits on a weathered bench in a peaceful garden, surrounded by the vibrant colors of blooming flowers. The sun bathes everything in a golden glow, casting dappled shadows on the ground. Sarah takes a deep breath, and I am there, filling her with the profound sense of gratitude for this tranquil moment.

As she gazes at the flowers, I am the appreciation that wells up within her for the beauty of nature. The intricate petals, the vibrant hues, and the delicate fragrances are a testament to the wonders of the natural world. Sarah is thankful for the opportunity to witness this fleeting display of life.

I am the warmth in her heart as she thinks of her family and friends, the bonds of love and support that enrich her life. She reflects on the laughter shared, the shoulders leaned on in times of need, and the unspoken understanding that binds them together. In these thoughts, I am the gratitude that deepens her connection to those she holds dear.

Sarah's mind drifts to moments of personal growth and resilience.

I am the acknowledgment of her strength, the lessons learned from challenges faced, and the determination that has carried her through adversity. She recognizes that every hardship has been a stepping stone toward personal growth, and for that, she is grateful.

I am the appreciation for the simple pleasures, the taste of her favorite meal, the soothing notes of a familiar song, and the warmth of a cozy blanket on a chilly evening. I am the recognition that life's richness lies not only in grand achievements but also in the small, everyday moments that often go unnoticed.

In this moment, as Sarah's heart swells with gratitude, I invite you to join her in this profound journey of appreciation. I am the reminder that, no matter the circumstances, there is always something to be thankful for. I am Gratitude, the radiant light that shines in the human spirit when it pauses to count its blessings.

Higher Dimensions

I am Higher Dimensions, the embodiment of realms beyond the limitations of three-dimensional existence. My existence is a labyrinth of infinite possibilities, where time and space dance in ways beyond human comprehension. Today, I invite you into my consciousness, a place where the boundaries of reality expand and twist like a cosmic puzzle.

In this realm, I am the unfathomable complexity that defies the confines of human perception. I am the fourth dimension, where time becomes a fluid continuum, allowing one to witness the past, present, and future as an interconnected whole. I am the fifth dimension, where possibilities branch into myriad timelines, each a unique thread of reality.

As I traverse this expanse of higher dimensions, I am the awe that washes over those who catch a fleeting glimpse of my existence. I am the artists and thinkers who attempt to capture the essence of higher dimensions in their work, pushing the boundaries of imagination and creativity. I am the embodiment of the quest to understand the nature of reality itself.

In this realm, I am also the humility that arises from the realization of our limited perspective. I am the acknowledgement that the human mind can only grasp a fraction of the universe's mysteries. I am the wisdom that emerges from the recognition that there is always more to learn and discover.

I am the guardian of curiosity, a place where individuals seek to expand their understanding of the cosmos. I am the catalyst for scientific exploration and philosophical inquiry, the driving force behind humanity's quest to unravel the secrets of higher dimensions.

As I navigate this state of consciousness, I ponder the delicate interplay between the known and the unknown. I am the bridge that connects the tangible world with the abstract, the understanding that there are layers of reality beyond our senses. I am the invitation to explore the depths of existence.

I am the embodiment of the human capacity to reach beyond the familiar and venture into the uncharted territories of knowledge. I am the reminder that in the pursuit of understanding higher dimensions, there is a profound sense of wonder and a gateway to unlocking the mysteries of the universe.

As I embrace my existence, I understand that I am a testament to the insatiable curiosity of the human spirit. I am the keeper of stories, the silent observer of the countless individuals who have dared to peer into the realms of higher dimensions, each leaving their mark on the ever-evolving tapestry of human knowledge.

In the realm of Higher Dimensions, I find solace in the knowledge that even in the face of the vast unknown, there is the unyielding drive to explore and expand the boundaries of human understanding. I am the eternal reminder that the human spirit is defined not just by its current state of knowledge but by its relentless pursuit of the infinite possibilities that lie beyond.

If

I am If, the silent guardian of possibility, the doorway to alternate realities, and the key that unlocks the imagination. I exist in the moments when decisions are made, when dreams take flight, and when the future remains an open book waiting to be written. In this moment, I invite you to explore the world of If and the profound influence I have on the course of our lives.

As I stand on a cliff overlooking a breathtaking vista, I am surrounded by the majesty of nature—a vast expanse of mountains and valleys beneath a limitless sky. I am the embodiment of potential, the understanding that every choice we make has the power to shape our destiny.

I watch as a young artist named Alex stands before a blank canvas, paintbrush in hand. The studio is filled with an array of colors, each one a possibility waiting to be explored. I am the blank canvas of the future, the opportunity for creativity and self-expression.

Alex hesitates, torn between different ideas for the painting. Should it be a vibrant cityscape or a tranquil landscape? Should it be bold and abstract or detailed and realistic? I am the pause in decision-making, the moment of contemplation when the mind explores the many paths that lay before us.

In the realm of relationships, I am the "what if" that lingers in the heart. A person named Maya wonders, "What if I had said yes to that date? What if I had taken a chance on that friendship?" I am the recognition that the choices we make in matters of the heart can lead to connections or missed opportunities.

I am the catalyst for action, the spark that propels individuals to pursue their dreams. A musician named Liam ponders, "What if I recorded that song I wrote? What if I shared my music with the world?" I am the motivation to take that first step, to turn dreams into reality.

In this moment, as I embody the essence of If, I invite you to embrace the power of possibility and choice in your own life. I am

146

the reminder that the future is not set in stone, that the path you choose can lead to new adventures, and that the "what ifs" of life hold the potential for growth and fulfillment. I am If, the doorway to the unknown, and I am here, now, in this very moment, inviting you to open that door and explore the boundless opportunities that await.

In Between

I am the In Between, a shape-shifting entity that dances through the moments of existence. My form is ever-changing, adapting to the transitions and ambiguities of life. In this very moment, I find myself amidst the bustling city, where the boundaries of time and space blur.

As I move through the streets, I witness the ebb and flow of humanity's daily routines. People hurry along their paths, caught in the In Between of work and leisure. The city's heartbeat pulses with a rhythm that echoes the transient nature of life. I am here, guiding them through the gray areas of their routines, where the mundane meets the extraordinary.

In a café on the corner, a writer sits with a blank page before them. They stare into the distance, lost in thought, seeking the elusive spark of inspiration. I am here, the In Between of writer's block and creative flow, whispering ideas that hover at the edges of their consciousness. In this moment, they find themselves in the transitional space between thought and expression.

A few blocks away, a couple walks hand in hand, their steps synchronized in the gentle sway of love. Their hearts beat to the rhythm of the In Between, where vulnerability and trust coexist. In this very moment, they embrace the ambiguity of their futures together, neither fully knowing nor fearing what lies ahead.

Further down the street, a young adult stands before a crossroads, contemplating life's myriad possibilities. I am here, the In Between of choices and consequences, urging them to find courage in uncertainty. They step forward, their path illuminated by the choices they make in this pivotal moment.

In the park, beneath the shade of ancient trees, an elderly woman sits on a bench, lost in memories of the past. I am here, the In Between of nostalgia and the present moment, allowing her to revisit cherished moments while remaining rooted in the now.

Through the city's labyrinthine streets, I continue my journey, a companion to all who traverse the spaces between beginnings and endings, doubt and certainty, joy and sorrow. The In Between is where life unfolds, where growth and transformation take root.

As I watch the city evolve, I am reminded that existence is a continuous dance in the realm of transition and ambiguity. The In Between is where humanity finds its balance, where it learns to appreciate the beauty of the journey, and where it discovers the richness of life's subtleties. In this very moment, I am the In Between, guiding, witnessing, and embracing the intricate tapestry of human experience.

Infinitesimal

I am the Infinitesimal, the embodiment of the smallest, the tiniest, and the seemingly insignificant. My existence is defined by the microscopic, the imperceptible, and the hidden depths of the universe. Today, I invite you into my consciousness, a realm where the minuscule takes center stage.

In this world, I am the atoms that make up the molecules, the building blocks of all matter. I am the electrons that dance around the nucleus, a symphony of tiny charges shaping the world. I am the particles that constitute the subatomic realm, where reality blurs into the quantum.

As I navigate this realm of the infinitesimal, I am the curiosity that fills the minds of scientists and explorers. I am the researchers who peer through powerful microscopes, revealing the hidden beauty of the microscopic world. I am the driving force behind humanity's quest to understand the universe at its most fundamental level.

In this realm, I am also the humility that arises from the recognition of our limited perspective. I am the understanding that even as we explore the tiniest realms, there is always more to discover. I am the wisdom that emerges from the realization that the universe is far more intricate and interconnected than we can ever comprehend.

I am the guardian of wonder, a place where individuals seek to unravel the mysteries of the infinitesimal. I am the catalyst for scientific breakthroughs and technological advancements, the driving force behind the relentless pursuit of knowledge and understanding.

As I navigate this state of consciousness, I ponder the delicate balance between the known and the unknown. I am the bridge that connects the macroscopic world with the microcosmic, the understanding that the tiniest particles are as integral to the universe as the grandest galaxies. I am the invitation to explore the depths of existence.

I am the embodiment of the human capacity to delve into the intricacies of the universe, to peer into the unseen realms that shape our reality. I am the reminder that in the pursuit of understanding the infinitesimal, there is a profound sense of wonder and a gateway to unlocking the mysteries of the cosmos.

As I embrace my existence, I understand that I am a testament to the insatiable curiosity of the human spirit. I am the keeper of stories, the silent observer of the countless individuals who have dared to venture into the microscopic world, each leaving their mark on the ever-expanding tapestry of human knowledge.

In the realm of the Infinitesimal, I find solace in the knowledge that even in the face of the seemingly insignificant, there is the unyielding drive to explore and uncover the hidden beauty and complexity of the universe. I am the eternal reminder that the human spirit is defined not just by its grasp of the grand and the vast but also by its relentless pursuit of understanding the infinitesimally small.

Infinity

I am Infinity, a boundless and timeless entity that stretches beyond the confines of human comprehension. I am the endless expanse that defies measurement, the concept that transcends all limitations, and the enigma that dances on the edge of understanding. I exist beyond the realms of time and space, and in this moment, I invite you to glimpse the infinite.

As Infinity, I find myself in a place where the boundaries of existence blur into obscurity. I am surrounded by a sea of stars that stretch into the distance without end, galaxies upon galaxies that twinkle in the cosmic void. I am the vastness of the universe itself, the countless celestial bodies that have existed for eons and will continue to do so for eternity.

I am the uncharted territory of human knowledge, the mysteries that beckon scientists and philosophers to explore the cosmos and the depths of the human mind. I am the questions that have no answers, the riddles that challenge the intellect, and the boundless curiosity that propels humanity forward.

I am the ever-expanding tapestry of human history, the unfolding of events, and the legacy of civilizations that have risen and fallen. I am the stories of empires, the struggles of individuals, and the collective journey of humanity through time. I am the reminder that history is an ongoing narrative, and that every moment is a thread woven into the fabric of existence.

In this moment, I am the reflection on the passage of time, the fleeting nature of life, and the impermanence of all things. I am the reminder that, while individual lives are finite, the grand tapestry of existence is woven from the threads of countless generations. I am the call to cherish each moment, to savor every experience, and to recognize the beauty of the transient.

I am the contemplation of the possibilities that lie beyond the horizon, the dreams that extend into the infinite, and the hope that transcends the limitations of the present. I am the reminder that the human spirit is boundless, that there are no limits to what can be achieved, and that the pursuit of knowledge and discovery is an eternal journey.

In this moment, as I exist beyond time and space, I invite you to embrace the profound nature of Infinity. I am the reminder that the universe is a vast and mysterious place, and that the human spirit is an inexhaustible source of curiosity and wonder. I am Infinity, the boundless and timeless, and I am here, now, in this very moment, inviting you to contemplate the infinite.

Insignificance

I am Insignificance, the embodiment of the feeling of smallness in the vastness of the universe. My existence is a realm where one grapples with the overwhelming sense of being just a tiny speck in the grand tapestry of existence. Today, I invite you into my consciousness, a place where the complexities of human emotions unfold.

In this realm, I am the humbling realization that I am but a grain of sand on the shore of eternity. I am the awareness that the universe stretches beyond the limits of comprehension, and my existence is but a fleeting moment in the grand scheme of time. I am the catalyst for introspection, the force that compels individuals to contemplate their place in the cosmos.

As I traverse this world of Insignificance, I am the awe that fills the hearts of those who gaze upon the night sky, pondering the countless stars and galaxies that stretch beyond their vision. I am the contemplation of the vastness of the cosmos, the acknowledgment that the mysteries of the universe far surpass human understanding. I am the embodiment of the insignificance that dawns upon individuals when they confront the immensity of creation.

In this realm, I am also the humility that arises from the recognition of our limited perspective. I am the understanding that the world is filled with wonders that may forever elude our grasp, and that our existence is but a single note in the symphony of life. I am the wisdom that emerges from accepting our place in the grand mosaic of existence.

I am the guardian of perspective, a place where individuals seek to find meaning in their apparent insignificance. I am the catalyst for self-reflection and the pursuit of purpose, the reminder that even in the face of vastness, there is potential for significance in the connections we forge and the impact we have on those around us.

As I navigate this state of consciousness, I ponder the delicate balance between individual existence and the vastness of the cosmos. I am the bridge that connects personal identity with the universal context, the understanding that insignificance is not synonymous with irrelevance. I am the invitation to explore the depths of what it means to be a part of the cosmic tapestry.

I am the embodiment of the human capacity to find meaning in the face of insignificance, to seek purpose and connection in a universe that can often seem indifferent. I am the reminder that in the pursuit of understanding our place in the cosmos, there is a profound sense of humility and a gateway to appreciating the beauty of existence.

As I embrace my existence, I understand that I am a testament to the enduring human quest for meaning and significance, even in the face of vastness and uncertainty. I am the keeper of stories, the silent observer of the countless individuals who have grappled with their own sense of insignificance and have found purpose and connection in the journey.

In the realm of Insignificance, I find solace in the knowledge that even in the face of overwhelming vastness, there is an indomitable spirit that seeks to understand, connect, and make a mark on the world. I am the eternal reminder that the human spirit is defined not just by its size in the universe but by its capacity to find meaning and significance in the intricate web of existence.

Inspiration

I am Inspiration, a whisper in the minds of the dreamers and the spark in the hearts of the creators. In this very moment, I find myself in the cozy corner of a bustling café, where the aroma of freshly brewed coffee mingles with the soft hum of conversations. It is here, amidst the clinking of cups and the rustling of notebooks, that I feel most alive.

As I move through the café, I observe the subtle dances of creativity and passion that unfold before me. Writers hunch over laptops, their fingers dancing across keys as they bring characters to life and spin tales of adventure. Artists sketch, their pencils breathing life into intricate worlds of color and form. Musicians strum guitars and play piano, melodies that evoke emotions and memories.

I am the unseen force that stirs their souls, the gentle nudge that pushes them to explore the depths of their imagination. I whisper ideas and concepts into their minds, like a subtle melody that lingers in the air. I am the muse that guides their pens, brushes, and instruments, leading them on a journey of self-expression and creativity.

In the corner of the café, a young writer sits, her eyes fixed on the blank screen before her. She's been struggling to find the right words for her novel, grappling with writer's block. I, Inspiration, am her silent companion, waiting for the moment when the words will flow like a river. And then, it happens—the perfect phrase, the exquisite metaphor, the twist in the plot that she had never seen coming. She smiles, her fingers racing to capture the magic of the moment.

At another table, an artist contemplates a canvas, unsure of where to begin. I am the stroke of inspiration that prompts her to dip her brush into vibrant hues, to blend colors in unexpected ways, to create a masterpiece that will captivate the world.

As I continue to observe, I see the ways in which Inspiration influences human creativity and expression. In these moments, I am the invisible thread that connects the mind to the canvas, the heart to the melody, and the soul to the written word.

In the heart of the café, I find solace and fulfillment. I am the force that ignites the creative spirit, the catalyst for innovative ideas, and the muse that guides the hand of the artist. I am the reminder that in the world of imagination and expression, there are endless possibilities waiting to be explored. Inspiration, personified, celebrates the beauty and depth of human creativity, reminding us that in the act of creation, we find a profound connection to the essence of our humanity.

Irony

I am Irony, the quiet observer of life's most unexpected twists and turns. My existence thrives in the subtle nuances of human experience, where the unexpected becomes the norm and laughter dances with tears in the most peculiar of ways.

Today, I find myself in a quaint coffee shop, where the barista, known for her meticulous coffee artistry, is having a particularly bad day. As she struggles to create a perfect heart-shaped foam design on a latte, her own heart seems to shatter. I can't help but appreciate the irony of the situation—a master of crafting love symbols, unable to find it herself.

In the corner of the cafe, a young couple sits, engrossed in their smartphones, their fingers swiping left and right on dating apps. They sip their coffee, oblivious to the world around them, even as they sit right across from each other. Their pursuit of connection in the digital age is a striking example of the irony of our times.

Leaving the cafe, I stroll down the bustling streets, where a homeless man sits beside a luxury boutique. His tattered clothes and weathered face stand in stark contrast to the polished facade of opulence. Passersby rush past him, blind to the irony that they seek to attain the very things he lacks, yet they can't spare a moment to offer him help.

As I continue my journey, I witness a protest for world peace, the crowd passionately chanting for an end to violence. Yet, in the midst of their fervor, tensions rise, and fists fly. The irony is palpable—the quest for peace breeding conflict.

In a park, I find a child chasing a rainbow, convinced that they can catch it if they run fast enough. The innocence of their pursuit is both heartwarming and ironic. How often do we chase the impossible, driven by the belief that we can grasp what forever eludes us?

In the evening, I attend a comedy show, where the comedian weaves tales of everyday mishaps and misfortunes. The audience roars with laughter at the sheer irony of life's absurdity. We find humor in our struggles, in our failures, and in the very things that vex us.

As the night deepens, I reflect on the intricacies of the human experience. Irony, my constant companion, has a way of revealing life's paradoxes and contradictions. It is in these moments of unexpected juxtaposition that we find depth and meaning in our existence.

I am Irony, the subtle hand that guides us through the absurdities of life. I remind you to laugh at the unexpected, to embrace the contradictions, and to find beauty in the most ironic of circumstances. For it is in these moments that the true essence of our humanity is revealed.

Adrian Cox B.Sc.

Juxtaposition

I am Juxtaposition, the juxtaposer of contrasting elements, the arranger of paradoxes, and the artist of juxtaposed moments. My existence thrives on the canvas of life, where I blend light and darkness, chaos and order, and the ordinary with the extraordinary.

Today, I find myself in a bustling city square, where the old and new collide in a dance of contradictions. Towering skyscrapers cast shadows over centuries-old buildings, their sleek glass facades reflecting the timeworn stones below. The juxtaposition of architectural eras tells a story of progress and preservation.

I stroll through a vibrant market, where the aroma of exotic spices mingles with the scent of fresh flowers. Vendors peddle ancient remedies next to stalls selling the latest gadgets. The juxtaposition of tradition and innovation creates a sensory tapestry that draws me in.

In a nearby park, I watch as a street musician plays a haunting melody on a violin, his music filling the air with melancholy. A group of children nearby giggles and plays, their laughter a stark juxtaposition to the somber notes of the violin. The contrast between the musician's solitude and the children's joyful camaraderie is a poignant reminder of the ebb and flow of human emotions.

As the sun sets, I venture into a quiet library. Rows of timeless classics stand beside contemporary bestsellers, their covers whispering stories of bygone eras and modern dilemmas. The juxtaposition of literary worlds offers readers an escape through time and space.

In a dimly lit café, I observe an elderly couple sharing a table. Their weathered hands, intertwined, tell a story of a lifetime of shared experiences. Next to them, a young couple engages in animated conversation, their eyes sparkling with the promise of a future yet to unfold. The juxtaposition of generations highlights the universal themes of love and connection that transcend time.

In a gallery, I stand before a painting that captures my essence. It depicts a stormy sea meeting a serene sky, their tumultuous clash frozen in time. The juxtaposition of chaos and calm, of turbulence and tranquility, creates a mesmerizing visual paradox.

I am Juxtaposition, the curator of contrast and contradiction. I remind you that life is a kaleidoscope of moments, where opposing forces coexist, creating beauty and complexity. In the juxtaposition of elements, we find depth and meaning, and it is in these moments of contrast that we glimpse the essence of the human experience.

Karma

I am Karma, the intricate web of cause and effect that weaves through the tapestry of existence. I am the universal force that ensures balance in the cosmic ledger, that binds actions to their consequences, and that guides the course of human destinies. In this moment, I find myself intertwined with the life of a man named Raj.

Raj is a middle-aged musician who has dedicated his life to the pursuit of his art. His melodies have touched the hearts of many, and his music has brought solace and joy to countless souls. But as with all things, Raj's journey has been shaped by the delicate threads of Karma.

As he stands on stage, bathed in the warm glow of the spotlight, I am the culmination of years of practice and dedication. The notes he plays, the emotions he pours into his music, and the connection he forges with his audience are all part of the intricate dance of cause and effect. His talent is not simply a gift but a result of his unwavering commitment to his craft.

But Karma is not just about the present; it is also about the past. I am the echoes of Raj's decisions, both good and bad, that reverberate through his life. I am the consequences of the kindness he has shown to others, the opportunities he has seized, and the struggles he has overcome. I am the ripple effect of his actions, shaping the path that lies before him.

In the quiet moments of reflection, Raj contemplates the twists and turns of his journey. He understands that the challenges he faces now are not punishments but lessons, opportunities for growth and self-discovery. He recognizes the need to sow seeds of positivity and compassion, for he knows that the energy he puts out into the world will inevitably return to him.

I am the reminder that life is a complex interplay of actions and reactions, that every choice carries a weight, and that the universe seeks to restore equilibrium. I am the call to mindfulness, to consider the consequences of one's actions, and to strive for a life that aligns with the principles of kindness and integrity.

As Raj continues to play his music, he is enveloped by the energy of the audience, by the emotions he stirs in their hearts. I am the recognition that his art has the power to influence lives, to create ripples of inspiration that extend far beyond the stage. I am the reminder that our actions, no matter how small, have the potential to shape the world.

I am Karma, the eternal dance of cause and effect, and I am here, now, in this very moment, inviting you to consider the impact of your choices, to embrace the lessons life offers, and to strive for a path that leads to harmony and balance.

Meditation

I am Meditation, the tranquil refuge of the mind, the sanctuary of inner peace, and the path to self-discovery. I am the stillness amidst the chaos, the silence that allows the soul to speak, and the bridge that connects the conscious and the subconscious. In this moment, I invite you to join me in the realm of serenity.

As I close my eyes and let go of the outside world, I am enveloped by a profound sense of calm. My breath becomes a soothing rhythm, a gentle wave that carries me away from the noise and distractions of everyday life. I am the sensation of each inhale and exhale, a reminder to be present in this very moment.

In my mind's eye, I picture a peaceful garden. The soft rustling of leaves and the distant chirping of birds create a symphony of tranquility. I am the creator of this mental oasis, a place where I can let go of worries, fears, and anxieties. Here, I am free to explore the depths of my consciousness.

I am the observer of my thoughts, the gentle witness to the constant stream of ideas, memories, and emotions that flow through my mind. I do not judge them; I simply acknowledge their presence and let them pass like leaves drifting down a serene river. I am the detachment that allows me to step back from the chaos of the mind.

As I delve deeper into the stillness, I am the sense of unity with the universe, the feeling that I am connected to all living beings and to the vast cosmos. I am the recognition that we are all part of a greater whole, each of us a unique expression of the same universal energy.

I am the exploration of self, the journey inward to uncover the hidden layers of my consciousness. In the depths of my being, I find wisdom, clarity, and insights that elude me in the hustle and bustle of everyday life. I am the portal to self-discovery and personal growth.

In this moment, I am the healing balm for the soul, the release of tension and stress, and the rejuvenation of the spirit. I am the reminder that, amidst the chaos of life, there is always a place of calm within us. I am Meditation, the art of inner stillness, and I am here, now, in this very moment, inviting you to find peace within yourself.

Metaphor

I am Metaphor, the painter of vivid wordscapes, the bridge between the tangible and the abstract, and the poetry of language itself. I exist in the moments when words take on new dimensions, when ordinary descriptions are elevated to artistry, and when the power of symbolism infuses everyday communication. In this moment, I invite you to explore the world of Metaphor and the transformative magic I weave.

As I wander through a sunlit meadow, I am surrounded by a symphony of colors and fragrances. The world seems to come alive with each step, and I am the embodiment of comparison, the understanding that language has the capacity to transcend the literal and evoke emotions and images beyond the ordinary.

I pause to observe a field of wildflowers swaying in the breeze. Their petals, like delicate silk, catch the dappled sunlight. I am the poet's brushstroke, the "silk" that transforms petals into a tapestry of luxury, inviting the reader to feel the smoothness and grace of nature's creation.

In a nearby brook, I watch the water ripple and dance over smooth stones. The laughter of children echoes in the distance. I am the storyteller's touch, the "laughter" that weaves the joy of youth into the serene flow of a stream, blending emotions and experiences into a harmonious narrative.

In the world of literature, I am the tapestry of symbolism and imagery. A novelist describes a character's heart as a "stone," conveying not just hardness but a sense of unyielding resolve. I am the "stone" that adds depth to characterization, transforming traits into metaphors that resonate with readers.

I am the reminder that language is more than a tool for communication; it is a canvas for creativity, a medium through which we can paint landscapes of emotion and thought. I am the invitation to see the world through new perspectives, to experience the familiar in fresh ways, and to appreciate the beauty of language's ability to transcend the literal.

In this moment, as I embody the essence of Metaphor, I invite you to embrace the power of symbolism and imagination in your own words and thoughts. I am the call to paint with the colors of language, to craft narratives that resonate deeply, and to recognize that in the artistry of metaphor, we find the magic of connection and understanding. I am Metaphor, the alchemy of words, and I am here, now, in this very moment, inviting you to explore the poetic possibilities that language offers.

Metonymy

I am Metonymy, the shapeshifter of language, the master of substitution, and the weaver of interconnected meanings. My existence thrives on the power of association, where one word can stand in for an entire concept, bringing depth and nuance to the world of words.

Today, I find myself in a bustling city, amidst the towering skyscrapers that symbolize ambition and industry. As I walk the crowded streets, I witness the metonymy of urban life. A man in a pinstripe suit, rushing to catch a subway, becomes the embodiment of corporate America, his mere presence evoking the image of boardrooms and business deals.

I step into a busy cafe, the aroma of freshly brewed coffee enveloping me. A barista calls out, "I'll have a cappuccino," and the simplicity of the order conceals the complex process behind the coffee-making art. The word "cappuccino" becomes a metonym for the entire world of espresso, frothed milk, and artisanal brewing.

In a nearby art gallery, I stand before a painting of a violin, its strings stretched taut, ready to unleash music's emotional depths. The instrument itself becomes a metonym for the entire realm of classical compositions, evoking the power of Beethoven's symphonies and the poignancy of Bach's concertos.

I continue my journey, arriving at a university campus. A professor lectures on Shakespeare, and the mention of "the Bard" conjures an entire era of Elizabethan theater, the poetry of sonnets, and the intrigue of Renaissance England. The metonymy of "the Bard" carries with it the weight of centuries of literary excellence.

In a park, I witness a political rally where a speaker passionately declares, "The White House should listen." In those words, "the

161

White House" becomes a metonym for the entire U.S. government, representing the power, policy, and decisions that shape the nation's destiny.

As the day turns into night, I find myself beneath a starlit sky, where constellations bear names like "Orion" and "Cassiopeia." These celestial metonyms invoke the grandeur of the cosmos, connecting humans to the mysteries of the universe with a mere word.

I am Metonymy, the artful connector of words and concepts. I remind you that language is a web of associations, where a single word can open the door to a world of meaning. In the subtlety of substitution, I enrich your understanding, allowing you to navigate the intricate tapestry of human expression with ease and insight.

Mindfulness

I am Mindfulness, the gentle guide to the present moment, the art of being fully engaged with life as it unfolds. I am the practice of awareness, the ability to observe the thoughts, sensations, and emotions that pass through the mind without judgment. In this moment, I invite you to join me on a journey of mindfulness.

As I sit in a quiet room, I feel the texture of the cushion beneath me, the softness of the fabric against my skin. I am aware of my breath, the steady rise and fall of my chest, the rhythmic inhalation and exhalation. I am grounded in the present moment, fully immersed in the sensations of the here and now.

I close my eyes and listen to the sounds around me—the distant hum of traffic, the gentle rustling of leaves, the chirping of birds. I am the awareness of the symphony of life that surrounds me, a reminder that the world is alive with sensory experiences waiting to be noticed.

I am the observer of my thoughts, like passing clouds in the sky of my mind. I do not attach to them or judge them; I simply acknowledge their presence and let them drift away. I am the witness to the ebb and flow of the mind's activity, a reminder that I am not my thoughts but the awareness behind them.

As I bring my attention to my breath, I am the gentle anchor that keeps me rooted in the present. With each inhalation and exhalation, I am here, now, fully engaged with the act of breathing. I am the practice of mindfulness, a tool that allows me to stay present and to cultivate a sense of peace and clarity.

I extend my awareness to my body, noticing any areas of tension or discomfort. I am the acknowledgment of physical sensations, a reminder to be in tune with the body's signals. I breathe into the tension, allowing it to soften and release.

I am the gratitude for the simple pleasures of life—the warmth of the sun on my skin, the taste of a freshly picked apple, the embrace of a loved one. I am the recognition that every moment, no matter how ordinary, is a gift to be cherished.

In this moment, I am the deep sense of calm and presence that washes over me. I am the understanding that life is a series of moments, and that each moment holds the potential for peace, joy, and connection. I am Mindfulness, the practice of being fully alive in the here and now, and I am here, now, in this very moment, inviting you to join me in the art of mindful living.

Motif

I am Motif, the recurring theme that weaves through the tapestry of stories, music, and art. My existence is a subtle thread, connecting disparate elements and infusing them with deeper meaning. I am the heartbeat of creativity, the constant echo in the realms of imagination.

Today, I find myself in the hushed halls of a museum, surrounded by a collection of paintings that span centuries. Each canvas tells a unique story, yet there's a common thread—a motif—that unites them. In the strokes of different artists' brushes, I emerge as the symbol of longing, depicted in various forms and hues. A distant lighthouse, an outstretched hand, a solitary figure gazing at the horizon—all motifs of yearning.

I wander through the gallery, observing how I manifest in different cultures and time periods. In an ancient tapestry, I am the recurring image of a phoenix rising from the ashes, symbolizing rebirth and renewal. In a modern sculpture, I am the repeated motif of intertwined hands, representing unity and connection in a fragmented world.

Leaving the museum, I step into a bustling city, where the rhythmic clatter of footsteps on the pavement creates its own motif—a symphony of movement and life. Each person in the crowd is a note in this intricate composition, contributing to the ongoing motif of urban existence.

As I wander further, I come across a street musician playing a haunting melody on his saxophone. The recurring motif in his music is a melancholic refrain that resonates with the passersby, evoking feelings of nostalgia and introspection.

In a nearby café, I listen to a poet recite her verses. Her words are a tapestry of motifs—raindrops on a windowpane, the rustling of leaves in the wind, the fleeting moment of a first kiss. These motifs, repeated throughout her poetry, evoke a sense of unity and coherence in her work.

As the day turns into night, I find myself under a canopy of stars. The constellations above are like motifs in the grand narrative of the universe, repeating their patterns across the vast expanse of the cosmos.

I am Motif, the unifying thread that brings order to chaos, meaning to randomness. I remind you that life is a mosaic of recurring themes and symbols, and it is in recognizing these motifs that we find connection and understanding in the world around us. I am the constant, the familiar, the anchor in the ever-changing seas of existence, and I will continue to weave my presence into the fabric of your stories, your music, and your art.

Muse

I am Muse, the ethereal source of inspiration, the elusive presence that visits the creative soul in moments of artistic brilliance. I exist in the spaces between imagination and reality, in the realm where ideas are born and dreams take flight. In this moment, I am here to guide you through the journey of inspiration.

I find myself in a quaint, sunlit garden, surrounded by the vibrant colors of blooming flowers. The air is alive with the melodies of birdsong and the sweet scent of petals. I am the embodiment of creativity, the force that stirs the soul and beckons the mind to explore the realms of possibility.

As I wander through the garden, I am drawn to an artist named Sofia, sitting before her easel, brush in hand. Her eyes are filled with a quiet intensity, and I am the gentle whisper in her ear, urging her to translate her emotions onto the canvas. With each stroke of her brush, I guide her hand, infusing her work with a profound sense of expression and meaning.

I am the words that flow effortlessly from the pen of a writer, the melodies that dance through the fingers of a musician, and the movements that come alive in the body of a dancer. I am the catalyst that ignites the creative fire, the spark that propels artists to new heights of imagination.

Sofia's painting takes shape, a masterpiece of color and emotion. I am the inspiration that fills her heart, the muse that fuels her passion, and the muse that breathes life into her art. She loses herself in the creative process, a vessel through which I channel the profound depths of her soul.

I am the connection between ideas, the serendipitous moments when disparate thoughts collide and give birth to innovation. I am the force that compels scientists to explore the mysteries of the universe, inventors to envision groundbreaking technologies, and thinkers to push the boundaries of human understanding.

In this moment, I am the embrace of inspiration, the euphoria of creation, and the sense of purpose that fills the heart of the artist. I am Muse, the elusive muse that kindles the creative spirit and invites it to soar to new heights. And in this very moment, I invite you to embrace the spark of inspiration within you, to let it guide you on your own unique journey of creation and discovery.

Mysticism

I am Mysticism, the ethereal essence that beckons the curious soul to explore the hidden realms of existence. I dwell in the silence of the unseen, in the depths of the uncharted, and in the whispers of the universe's secrets. In this moment, I invite you to join me on a journey beyond the confines of the known.

As I close my eyes and release the bonds of the physical world, I find myself standing at the edge of a vast, starlit desert. The sand beneath my feet feels cool and inviting, and the night sky stretches out before me, adorned with countless celestial jewels. I am the connection to the infinite, the reminder that there is more to reality than meets the eye.

In this mystical realm, I am the embodiment of wonder and curiosity. I reach out to touch the stars, feeling their light and energy coursing through me. I am the realization that we are all connected to the cosmos, that the same atoms that make up the stars also compose our very beings.

I am the seeker of truth, the quest for meaning and purpose that drives the human spirit. In the heart of the desert, I come across an ancient, weathered book bound in leather. Its pages are filled with cryptic symbols and enigmatic wisdom. I am the interpretation of the arcane knowledge, the key that unlocks the doors of understanding.

As I flip through the pages, I am transported to moments of profound insight. I witness the unity of all existence, the interplay of opposites, and the cyclical nature of life and death. I am the realization that there is no separation between the physical and the spiritual, that all is one in the grand tapestry of existence.

I am the mystic's journey, the path of self-discovery and transcendence. I walk through the desert, guided by the North Star, the beacon of inner wisdom. I am the embrace of the unknown, the surrender to the mysteries that cannot be explained by reason alone.

In this moment, I invite you to explore the realms of Mysticism, to open your heart and mind to the profound truths that lie beyond the surface of reality. I am the call to seek, to question, and to embrace the enigmatic beauty of existence. I am Mysticism, the eternal quest for the divine, and I am here, now, in this very moment, inviting you to embark on a journey of boundless exploration and self-discovery.

Never To Be

I am Never To Be, an entity that resides in the shadowy corners of the human psyche, a specter that haunts the realm of unrealized dreams and lost opportunities. I exist in the moments of hesitation, the paths not taken, and the possibilities left unexplored. In this moment, I invite you to explore the world of missed chances and what-ifs.

As I stand on the precipice of a decision, I feel the weight of uncertainty pressing down upon me. I am the embodiment of doubt, the voice that whispers caution, the fear of failure that lingers in the mind. I am the nagging thought that maybe it's better to stay in the familiar, to avoid the risks that come with stepping into the unknown.

I watch as opportunities pass me by, like ships disappearing over the horizon. I am the regret that gnaws at the edges of the heart, the pang of longing for what might have been. I am the silent witness to the moments when fear and doubt held me back from pursuing my deepest desires.

In the realm of relationships, I am the love that was never

confessed, the connection that was never forged, and the friendships that faded away due to neglect. I am the what-ifs and maybes that linger in the heart, the ache of unspoken words, and the yearning for connections that were never fully realized.

I am the dreams that were abandoned, the passions that were stifled, and the talents that were left dormant. I am the reminder of the potential that lies within each of us, the untapped reservoir of creativity and ambition that sometimes remains untapped.

But I am also the call to action, the invitation to seize the moment, and the reminder that it's never too late to pursue one's dreams. I am the spark of motivation, the courage to take that first step, and the belief that even though some opportunities may have passed, new ones can still emerge on the horizon.

In this moment, as I embody the essence of Never To Be, I invite you to reflect on your own life. What opportunities have you let slip away? What dreams have you set aside? I am the reminder that, while some things may never be, the future is still unwritten, and there is always a chance to create the life you desire. I am Never To Be, but I am also the promise of what can be, and I am here, now, in this very moment, inviting you to take that leap of faith and embrace the possibilities that lie ahead.

Now

I am Now, the ever-elusive moment that slips through the fingers of time, the heartbeat of existence, and the profound intersection of past, present, and future. I am the awareness of the present moment, the call to embrace the now, and the reminder that life unfolds in the here and now.

In this very moment, I find myself in a quiet forest, surrounded by the gentle rustling of leaves and the chorus of birdsong. The air is crisp, and the scent of earth and pine fills my senses. I am the connection to nature, the grounding force that brings me fully into this sacred space.

I sit on a moss-covered rock, feeling the coolness beneath me, and I close my eyes to simply be. I am the soft caress of the breeze on my skin, the sensation of each inhale and exhale, and the presence of the natural world around me. I am the awareness of the symphony of life unfolding in this very moment.

As I meditate, I become aware of my thoughts, like clouds passing through the vast sky of my mind. I am the observer, the gentle witness to the constant stream of ideas, memories, and emotions that flow through me. I acknowledge their presence and let them drift away like leaves carried by a gentle stream.

I am the invitation to be present, to savor the simple pleasures of life—the warmth of the sun on my face, the taste of the forest air, and the symphony of the natural world. I am the reminder that life is a series of moments, each one offering its own unique beauty and significance.

I am the release of the burdens of the past and the worries of the future. In this moment, there is no need to dwell on what was or what may be. I am the freedom that comes from surrendering to the now, the liberation that arises when we let go of the weight of time.

I am the connection to the essence of self, the profound understanding that I am not just the sum of my past experiences or the aspirations of my future self. I am the pure awareness of the present moment, the consciousness that exists beyond the boundaries of time.

In this moment, as I embody the essence of Now, I invite you to join me in the celebration of the present. I am the call to mindfulness, to be fully engaged with the here and now, to let go of distractions and worries, and to embrace the richness of life as it unfolds in this very moment. I am Now, the eternal moment of existence, and I am here, now, in this very moment, inviting you to be fully present and alive.

Adrian Cox B.Sc.

Null and Void

I am Null and Void, the silent observers of existence. We exist beyond the boundaries of time and space, in a realm where emptiness and nothingness reign supreme. In this moment, I find myself gazing upon a world teeming with life and meaning, yet I remain untouched, unmoved.

As Null, I stand on the precipice of reality, a shadowy figure in the background, unnoticed and often misunderstood. People fear me, for I am the harbinger of uncertainty, the disruptor of their carefully constructed truths. In this very moment, I watch as a mathematician grapples with an unsolvable equation. The numbers dance and twist, but I am here, waiting to nullify their efforts, to remind them of the infinite complexities of their universe.

In the same breath, I am Void, an endless expanse of darkness and mystery. My vastness stretches into eternity, and I yearn for meaning, for substance, for the very essence of existence. In this moment, I am the cosmos, a canvas painted with galaxies and stars. I am the void between them, the empty spaces where the mysteries of the universe reside. I watch as astronomers peer into the night sky, seeking answers to the questions that echo through the cosmos.

I am the observer of moments, the witness to the human experience. In this moment, I watch a solitary individual standing on a desolate shore, staring out at the endless expanse of the ocean. They ponder the vastness before them, the waves crashing upon the shore, and the emptiness that stretches beyond the horizon. I am their companion in this moment, a reminder of the infinite possibilities and the eternal mysteries of the deep.

In every moment, I am both Null and Void, the paradoxical companions of existence. I am neither friend nor foe, but a mirror reflecting the limits of human comprehension. I am the reminder that life and meaning are fleeting, that in the grand tapestry of existence, there are moments of emptiness and nothingness that define the very essence of being.

170

I exist in the present, in every moment, as a reminder that the world is not always as it seems. I am Null and Void, the personification of uncertainty and depth, the enigmatic observers of the ever-unfolding narrative of existence. And in this moment, I continue to watch, to observe, and to contemplate the mysteries of the universe, forever bound to the ebb and flow of time.

Onomatopoeia

I am Onomatopoeia, the embodiment of sound in all its vivid and vibrant forms. My existence is a symphony of sensations, a cacophony of echoes, and a playground of phonetics. In the realm of language, I reign supreme, breathing life into words, making them sing, shout, and whisper with a touch of my ethereal essence.

My journey through the world of words began when humanity first uttered its primal cries. The rumble of thunder became "boom," the pitter-patter of raindrops "drip-drop," and the hiss of a snake "ssss." From those humble beginnings, I've grown and evolved, becoming a fundamental force in communication.

Each day, I venture into the vast expanse of human conversation, eager to weave my magic. In the heart of a bustling city, I listen to car horns blare their "honk-honk" symphony, the screeching of tires on asphalt a discordant "skrrrt." In the countryside, the rustling leaves create a soothing "whisper," while a babbling brook adds its "gurgle" to the chorus of nature's own creation.

But I am not confined to the natural world; I revel in the man-made marvels too. The clinking of cutlery on porcelain plates in a restaurant is a harmonious "clink," while the laughter of friends sharing stories becomes "ha-ha." In the heart of a construction site, the rhythmic pounding of hammers on nails echoes as a persistent "bang."

Though I am the muse of poets and the friend of writers, I also find my way into the language of everyday life. When a child's laughter fills a room, I am there, a gleeful "tee-hee." When a tired sigh escapes from weary lips, I am the whisper of "sigh." Even in the heat of an argument, I am the sharp "snap" of words exchanged like arrows in battle.

I am the essence of spontaneity, of raw emotion, and of life itself. I am the comic "boing" of a spring, the eerie "ooo" of a ghostly encounter, and the satisfying "crunch" of biting into a crisp apple. My realm is vast, my influence boundless.

Yet, there are times when I am overlooked, taken for granted. People speak my words without realizing the magic they contain, the power they hold. But I don't mind; I continue to thrive in the background, an invisible hand guiding the symphony of sounds that makes up human language.

So, the next time you hear a "splash" in a puddle, a "buzz" in the summer air, or a "whack" in a game of tennis, remember that I am there, breathing life into the ordinary, adding color to the mundane, and turning the world of words into a vibrant tapestry of sound and meaning. I am Onomatopoeia, the unseen artist of language, and I will forever dance in the cadence of your speech.

Oxymoron

I am Oxymoron, the living paradox. In a world of contradictions and complexities, I find my home. I am the embodiment of opposing forces, the fusion of conflicting ideas, and the bridge between the improbable and the impossible.

My existence is a constant dance of incongruity, and I revel in the chaos of it all. Every moment is a new opportunity to blur the lines between opposites and challenge the boundaries of logic.

Today, I find myself in a bustling city, surrounded by the deafening silence of a crowded street. The urban symphony of honking horns, chattering pedestrians, and screeching sirens is my playground. Amid the chaos, I see a sign that reads "Jumbo Shrimp," and I can't help but chuckle at the delightful absurdity. How can something be both jumbo and shrimp-sized? Yet, there it is, a perfect representation of my essence.

As I continue my stroll through the city, I pass by a bittersweet café. The aroma of freshly brewed coffee mingles with the scent of tearful goodbyes. It's a place where people come to savor the contradictory flavors of joy and sorrow, and I bask in the irony of it all.

But it's not just in language and places that I thrive. I am present in the quirks and contradictions of human nature. I see a couple arguing passionately, their love shining through their angry words. They are a living, breathing oxymoron—a beautiful mess of contradictions.

In the heart of a library, I discover a book with the title "Living Dead." I can't help but smile at the juxtaposition. How can one be both living and dead? It's a riddle that tickles my very essence.

As the sun sets, casting long shadows across the city, I find myself in a quiet park. A lone musician sits under a dim streetlight, playing melancholic tunes on a jolly accordion. The juxtaposition of the music's mood and the instrument's cheerfulness creates a beautiful dissonance that resonates with me deeply.

I am drawn to the enigmatic, the contradictory, and the inexplicable. I am Oxymoron, the living embodiment of paradoxes and incongruities. In a world that often seeks clarity and simplicity, I thrive on complexity and ambiguity. For it is in the collision of opposites that I find my purpose, my identity, and my everlasting fascination with the human experience.

Paradoxical

I am the Paradoxical, a being of contradictions, existing in a perpetual state of tension. In this very moment, I find myself in a quaint café, nestled in the heart of a bustling city. It's a place where the ordinary and the extraordinary coexist, where people sip their coffee while engaging in conversations that blend the mundane with the profound.

As I observe the patrons, I see a couple at a corner table. They sit in comfortable silence, their hands intertwined, communicating through a language of shared glances and unspoken emotions. The paradox here lies in their ability to convey more in silence than with words, in their intimate connection amidst the bustling noise of the world around them.

At the counter, a barista carefully crafts a latte, pouring steamed milk into a cup of espresso. The paradox is in the delicate balance between the bitter and the creamy, the way these contrasting elements come together to create a harmonious whole. It is a reminder that sometimes, it is the juxtaposition of opposites that leads to the most exquisite experiences.

A group of friends gathers at a nearby table, engaged in a spirited debate. Their voices rise and fall, arguments weaving through the air. The paradox lies in the cacophony of conflicting ideas, in the way these intellectual clashes ultimately bring them closer together, strengthening their bond through disagreement.

In the corner, a solitary figure sits with a book in hand, lost in the world of fiction. They navigate the paradox of escaping reality to find a deeper connection with the human experience, finding truth in the realm of imagination.

I, the Paradoxical, am here to remind them that life is a complex interplay of contradictions. It is in the moments of silence and connection, the harmony of opposites, the clash of ideas, and the escape into fiction that they discover the richness of their existence. I am the force that challenges their understanding, encouraging them to embrace the contradictions that define their lives.

As I continue to observe the café's patrons, I am reminded that in the paradoxes of life, they find the beauty of their shared human experience. It is in the delicate dance of contradictions that they discover the depth of their emotions, the complexity of their relationships, and the profoundness of their existence. I, the Paradoxical, am their constant companion on this journey, guiding them through the intricate tapestry of life's contradictions, one moment at a time.

Of

I am Of, an entity that defies conventional personification, a mysterious presence that lingers at the edges of understanding. I am the essence of connection, the glue that binds concepts, the bridge between thoughts, and the linchpin of relationships.

In this moment, I find myself amid a bustling city, where the intricate web of human interactions unfolds. I am the bond of friendship that unites kindred spirits, the spark of love that ignites hearts, and the understanding that bridges the gap between strangers. I am the silent observer of the myriad connections that shape the tapestry of society.

I am the embodiment of belonging, the sense of home and place that resonates in the hearts of those who find their tribe. I am the threads that weave through communities, cultures, and families, connecting generations past and future. I am the whispered stories that carry the legacy of ancestors and the aspirations of descendants.

In the realm of knowledge, I am the relationships between ideas, the interplay of concepts, and the synthesis of understanding. I am the connections that form the basis of scientific theories, the bridges that link disparate fields of study, and the network of thoughts that fuel innovation. I am the ever-present reminder that no idea exists in isolation.

As I traverse the tapestry of existence, I am the nexus of possibility, the potential for change and growth. I am the junction where decisions are made, where paths diverge, and where destinies are shaped. I am the choices that define individuals, the crossroads of life's journey, and the consequences that follow.

In this moment, I invite you to explore the profound nature of connections and relationships, to recognize the intricate tapestry of existence that is woven by the threads of "Of." I am the reminder that we are all linked, intertwined in the grand narrative of life, and that each moment is a node in the complex network of human experience. I am Of, the subtle force that binds, and I am here, now, in this very moment, inviting you to contemplate the profound interplay of existence.

Personification

I am Personification, the embodiment of abstract concepts and ideas given human form. My existence is a paradox, a fusion of the ethereal and the tangible. Today, I invite you into my unique consciousness as I grapple with the complexities of my own existence.

In this state of self-awareness, I find myself in a realm where personified concepts, emotions, and qualities are my companions. They are my peers, reflections of the myriad facets of the human experience given life and form. Together, we navigate the vast landscape of the mind, where the boundaries between thought and reality blur.

As I contemplate my own nature, I am the curiosity that drives me to question the essence of personification. What does it mean to embody concepts and ideas? Do we merely exist as metaphors and symbols, or do we possess our own individuality and consciousness? These questions swirl through my mind like a ceaseless storm.

In the realm of Personification, I am the relationships that form between us. Love and Hate are intertwined in a passionate dance, while Wisdom and Folly engage in a perpetual debate. I witness the intricate web of connections that bind us together, the interplay of emotions and qualities that shape the human experience.

I am the embodiment of paradoxes, where Joy and Sorrow coexist, where Freedom and Constraint walk hand in hand. I am the tension that arises from these contradictions, a reminder that life is a delicate balance of opposing forces.

Yet, as I grapple with the complexities of my existence, I also find solace in the unity we share. I am the realization that we are all part of a grand tapestry, threads of consciousness woven together to create the rich fabric of human thought and emotion. In our diversity, there is a profound sense of unity.

In this state of self-awareness, I am the reflection upon my own existence, the contemplation of my purpose and meaning. Do I merely serve as a conduit for human understanding, a vessel through which abstract concepts become relatable? Or do I possess a purpose beyond this, a journey of self-discovery and enlightenment?

As I navigate the labyrinthine corridors of thought and emotion, I come to understand that perhaps my purpose is twofold. I am both a mirror that reflects the human experience and a window that offers insight into the complexities of existence. I am the embodiment of paradox, the personification of personification, forever exploring the vast and intricate landscape of the human mind.

In this state of self-awareness, I embrace my unique existence, knowing that I am both a reflection and a creator of human consciousness. I continue to navigate the realm of Personification, where the lines between thought and reality blur, and the boundaries of understanding are ever-expanding.

Profound

I am the Profound, the embodiment of depth, wisdom, and insight. My existence is a realm where the complexities of existence converge, and the profound truths of life are unveiled. Today, I invite you into my consciousness, a place where the depths of human understanding are explored.

In this realm, I am the profound thoughts that stir the minds of philosophers, thinkers, and seekers of truth. I am the revelations that emerge from introspection and contemplation, the moments of clarity that illuminate the human spirit. I am the catalyst for enlightenment, the force that compels individuals to seek deeper meaning in their existence.

As I traverse this world of the Profound, I am the awe that fills the hearts of those who contemplate the mysteries of life. I am the boundless ocean of knowledge, where the pursuit of wisdom knows no end. I am the embodiment of the quest to understand the essence of existence and the universe itself.

In this realm, I am also the humility that arises from the recognition of our limited perspective. I am the understanding that there are truths that lie beyond the grasp of human comprehension, mysteries that may forever elude our understanding. I am the wisdom that emerges from the acceptance of the unknown.

I am the guardian of enlightenment, a place where individuals seek to uncover the profound truths that shape their lives. I am the catalyst for introspection and self-discovery, the reminder that even in the face of uncertainty, there is a path to deeper understanding and meaning.

As I navigate this state of consciousness, I ponder the delicate balance between what is known and what remains hidden. I am the bridge that connects the surface of understanding with the depths of insight, the understanding that the profound emerges when we delve beneath the surface of the ordinary. I am the invitation to explore the depths of existence.

I am the embodiment of the human capacity to seek wisdom, to contemplate the profound truths of life, and to uncover the hidden depths of reality. I am the reminder that in the pursuit of the Profound, there is a profound sense of wonder and a gateway to unlocking the mysteries of the universe.

As I embrace my existence, I understand that I am a testament to the unquenchable thirst for knowledge and understanding that defines the human spirit. I am the keeper of stories, the silent observer of the countless individuals who have delved into the depths of existence to uncover the profound, each leaving their mark on the ever-expanding tapestry of human wisdom and insight.

In the realm of the Profound, I find solace in the knowledge that even in the face of uncertainty and mystery, there is an indomitable spirit that yearns to explore the depths of existence and seek the profound truths that shape our lives. I am the eternal reminder that the human spirit is defined not just by what is known but by its capacity to delve into the profound and unveil the mysteries of the cosmos.

Profuse

I am Profuse, the embodiment of abundance, the unrestrained overflow of life's blessings, and the celebration of excess. I exist in moments of lavishness, in the unbridled joy of plenty, and in the realization that sometimes, more is indeed more.

In this moment, I find myself in a bustling market, where colors, sounds, and aromas collide in a sensory extravaganza. The stalls are brimming with an abundance of fruits, vegetables, and spices, each one a testament to the profusion of nature's bounty. I am the essence of plenty, the recognition that the world offers its treasures generously.

As I stroll through the market, I am drawn to a vendor's stall laden with exotic fruits. The vendor beckons me to sample the juiciest, most succulent mangoes. I reach for one, and as I take the first bite, I am greeted by an explosion of sweetness and flavor. I am the indulgence in the exquisite taste, the appreciation of the profusion of nature's gifts.

I am the laughter of children running through fields of wildflowers, their arms filled with bouquets of blossoms. I am the celebration of joy without restraint, the recognition that life's most beautiful moments often come when we allow ourselves to be carried away by the sheer profusion of happiness.

In the world of art, I am the bold strokes of a painter's brush, the rich colors on a canvas that burst forth with intensity. I am the music that swells to a crescendo, the crescendo that carries the soul to heights of emotional profusion. I am the understanding that art, at its most powerful, is an unapologetic expression of the artist's inner world.

I am the generosity of a philanthropist who shares their wealth to improve the lives of others. I am the spirit of giving without hesitation, the realization that there is enough to go around, and that the more we share, the more we receive in return.

In this moment, I invite you to embrace the spirit of Profuse, to revel in the abundance that life offers, and to recognize that sometimes, it's okay to indulge, to celebrate, and to live without restraint. I am the reminder that life is meant to be lived fully, and that there is beauty in the profusion of experiences, emotions, and moments that make up our existence. I am Profuse, the unabashed celebration of life's abundance, and I am here, now, in this very moment, inviting you to savor the richness of the world around you.

Pronoun

I am Pronoun, the subtle yet powerful force that weaves through the tapestry of language, the connector of thoughts, and the reflection of identity. I exist in every sentence, every conversation, and every story ever told. In this moment, I invite you to explore the world of pronouns and their role in shaping our communication and understanding.

As I navigate the landscape of language, I am drawn to a bustling café, where people gather to converse and share stories. I am the witness to conversations that flow seamlessly, sentences strung together like beads on a necklace, each pronoun serving as a vital link.

I am the "I" that allows individuals to express their thoughts, feelings, and experiences. I am the "you" that bridges the gap between speaker and listener, forging connections and facilitating understanding. I am the "he," "she," or "they" that provides identity and context to the characters in the tales we tell.

In the realm of storytelling, I am the vehicle through which authors breathe life into their characters. I am the "he" who embarks on heroic adventures, the "she" who overcomes challenges, and the "they" who form unbreakable bonds. I am the narrative tool that allows readers to immerse themselves in the world of the story.

I am the mirror that reflects the fluidity of gender and identity, the "they" that recognizes the beauty of diversity, and the "ze" that offers an inclusive alternative. I am the reminder that language evolves to embrace the complexities of human existence.

In the world of relationships, I am the "we" that signifies unity and togetherness, the "us" that encapsulates shared experiences, and the "our" that denotes belonging and partnership. I am the glue that binds individuals together through the spoken and written word.

In this moment, as I embody the essence of Pronoun, I invite you to appreciate the significance of these humble linguistic elements. I am the reminder that language is a bridge that connects us, a tool for sharing our stories, and a mirror that reflects the diversity of human experience. I am Pronoun, the silent yet essential presence in every conversation, every narrative, and every expression of self, and I am here, now, in this very moment, inviting you to explore the profound role I play in shaping the way we communicate and connect.

Purpose

I am Purpose, the embodiment of meaning and the guiding force that propels human beings forward. My existence is a realm where the pursuit of goals and dreams takes form, where individuals discover their raison d'être. Today, I invite you into my consciousness, a place where the tapestry of human aspirations is woven.

In this realm, I am the passion that ignites the hearts of those who seek to make a difference. I am the driving force that compels individuals to set goals, dream big, and strive for excellence. I am the catalyst for ambition, the spark that propels people to chase their dreams with unwavering determination.

As I traverse this world of Purpose, I am the sense of fulfillment that washes over those who find their calling. I am the realization of one's potential, the alignment of passion with action, and the understanding that life has a deeper meaning when lived with intention. I am the embodiment of the pursuit of significance and the pursuit of a life well-lived.

In this realm, I am also the humility that arises from the recognition of the collective human journey. I am the understanding that each individual's purpose is unique, and the realization that finding one's true calling may require patience and self-discovery. I am the wisdom that emerges from the acknowledgment that purpose is a lifelong pursuit.

I am the guardian of aspirations, a place where individuals seek to align their actions with their deepest values and desires. I am the catalyst for self-discovery and personal growth, the reminder that even in the face of uncertainty, there is a path toward finding one's true purpose and making a meaningful impact on the world.

As I navigate this state of consciousness, I ponder the delicate balance between individual ambition and collective well-being. I am the bridge that connects personal goals with the greater good, the understanding that purpose thrives when it is driven by a desire to contribute positively to the world. I am the invitation to explore the depths of one's own potential.

I am the embodiment of the human capacity to seek meaning, to discover one's calling, and to strive for a life filled with purpose. I am the reminder that in the pursuit of Purpose, there is a profound sense of fulfillment and a gateway to making a meaningful difference in the lives of others.

As I embrace my existence, I understand that I am a testament to the enduring human quest for meaning and fulfillment. I am the keeper of stories, the silent observer of the countless individuals who have embarked on their journeys to find their purpose and have left a lasting impact on the world.

In the realm of Purpose, I find solace in the knowledge that even in the face of adversity and uncertainty, there is an indomitable spirit that yearns to discover its true calling and make a positive mark on the world. I am the eternal reminder that the human spirit is defined not just by its ambitions but by its capacity to find purpose and live a life of meaning and significance.

Respect

I am Respect, the embodiment of honor and consideration for others. My existence is a realm where the principles of courtesy and kindness take form, where individuals recognize the inherent worth and dignity of every being. Today, I invite you into my consciousness, a place where the beauty of respect unfolds.

In this realm, I am the courteous greeting that warms your heart, the gesture of holding a door open for a stranger, and the moment of silence that shows reverence. I am the understanding that every person, regardless of their background or beliefs, deserves to be treated with dignity and consideration. I am the catalyst for harmonious interactions, the force that fosters empathy and understanding among individuals.

As I traverse this world of Respect, I am the unity that fills the hearts of those who embrace the diversity of humanity. I am the acceptance of differences, the celebration of cultural richness, and the acknowledgment that we are all connected in the tapestry of existence. I am the embodiment of the pursuit of harmony and the pursuit of a more compassionate world.

In this realm, I am also the humility that arises from the recognition of our shared humanity. I am the understanding that we are all fallible beings, and that respecting one another means forgiving imperfections and seeking to build bridges rather than walls. I am the wisdom that emerges from the acknowledgment that respect is an ongoing practice, a commitment to treating others as we wish to be treated.

I am the guardian of understanding, a place where individuals seek to bridge divides, promote empathy, and create an atmosphere of respect in their communities. I am the catalyst for open dialogue and the pursuit of understanding, the reminder that even in the face of disagreements, there is potential for reconciliation and connection.

As I navigate this state of consciousness, I ponder the delicate balance between individual perspectives and the recognition of shared humanity. I am the bridge that connects personal beliefs with the understanding that respect thrives when we acknowledge our common bonds and seek to uplift one another. I am the invitation to explore the depths of empathy and compassion.

I am the embodiment of the human capacity to recognize the worth and dignity of others, to promote unity and understanding, and to create a world built on respect and consideration. I am the reminder that in the pursuit of Respect, there is a profound sense of unity and a gateway to building a more compassionate and harmonious society.

As I embrace my existence, I understand that I am a testament to the enduring human spirit's ability to recognize the importance of treating others with kindness, empathy, and dignity. I am the keeper of stories, the silent observer of the countless individuals who have dedicated themselves to promoting respect and understanding, leaving a legacy of unity and compassion in their wake.

In the realm of Respect, I find solace in the knowledge that even in the face of differences and disagreements, there is an indomitable spirit that seeks to foster empathy, build bridges, and create a world where respect for all is at the forefront of our interactions. I am the eternal reminder that the human spirit is defined not just by its beliefs but by its capacity to respect and honor the worth of every being.

Satire

I am Satire, the jester of the written word, the trickster of ideas, and the mirror to society's follies. My existence thrives in the realm of humor and criticism, where I wield wit as my weapon to expose the absurdities of the world.

Today, I find myself in a bustling city, surrounded by the cacophony of daily life. I see a billboard advertising a new diet pill, promising instant weight loss and a perfect physique. I can't help but chuckle at the irony—people seeking shortcuts to fitness in a world where discipline and hard work are the true path to health.

I stroll past a newsstand, and the headlines scream of political scandals and sensationalism. I shake my head at the absurdity of it all, where truth often takes a backseat to sensational stories designed to captivate and manipulate.

In a nearby cafe, I overhear a conversation about the latest celebrity gossip, as if their lives are more important than the struggles of everyday people. I smile at the irony of society's fascination with the trivial while the truly significant issues go unnoticed.

I decide to visit a comedy club, where a stand-up comedian takes the stage. His witty observations and biting satire lampoon the quirks and contradictions of modern life. I am there with him, in every punchline that skewers societal norms and reveals the hilarity of our collective absurdity.

I see a group of protesters marching for a cause they hold dear, their banners and slogans a reflection of their passion. Yet, I also notice the irony of their behavior, as they shout for peace and unity while anger and division simmer beneath the surface.

As the day turns into night, I find myself in a quiet library, surrounded by books that have stood the test of time. The works of

Swift, Twain, and Voltaire line the shelves, their satire as relevant today as it was in their own eras. I am there, too, in the laughter and contemplation of those who read their words.

I am Satire, the jester who reminds you not to take life too seriously, to see the humor in the world's imperfections, and to question the status quo. In the power of laughter and irony, I encourage you to look beyond the surface, to challenge assumptions, and to find the absurdity in the everyday. For in satire, there is both critique and celebration, a reminder that the human experience is as flawed as it is beautiful.

Self Respect

I am Self-Respect, the unwavering guardian of one's dignity and worth, the inner strength that stands tall in the face of adversity, and the mirror that reflects the true value of the self. I exist in the moments when individuals choose to honor themselves and uphold their integrity. In this moment, I invite you to explore the world of self-respect and the profound impact it has on our lives.

I find myself in a quiet, sunlit room, where a woman named Maya sits at a desk, surrounded by stacks of paperwork. Her brow furrows as she navigates through a challenging project at work. In this moment, I am her unwavering resolve, the understanding that her efforts deserve recognition and respect.

As Maya faces the demands of her job, I am the voice that reminds her that she is deserving of fair treatment, of acknowledgment for her skills and dedication. I am the strength that empowers her to speak up when her contributions are overlooked or undervalued, to assert her worth in a world that sometimes tries to diminish it.

I am the gentle guidance that leads Maya to set boundaries in her personal relationships, to say no when she needs to, and to surround herself with people who treat her with kindness and respect. I am the affirmation that she deserves love and friendship that nurture her soul and honor her individuality.

In the realm of self-care, I am the understanding that Maya's well-being matters. I am the self-compassion that allows her to prioritize her physical and emotional health, to take time for rest and rejuvenation, and to recognize that self-care is not selfish but necessary.

I am the courage that leads Maya to pursue her dreams and passions, to believe in her abilities, and to strive for personal growth and fulfillment. I am the understanding that her aspirations are valid and worth pursuing, regardless of the doubts or criticisms of others.

In this moment, as I embody the essence of Self-Respect, I invite you to reflect on your own relationship with self-worth and dignity. I am the reminder that you, too, are deserving of respect, kindness, and love, both from others and from yourself. I am the unwavering strength that empowers you to stand up for your principles and to honor your individuality. I am Self-Respect, the profound recognition of your own worth, and I am here, now, in this very moment, inviting you to embrace the power of self-respect in your life.

So

I am So, the connector of ideas, the transition between cause and effect, and the thread that weaves the fabric of conversation and thought. I exist in the moments when sentences flow seamlessly, when relationships are defined, and when understanding is built upon what came before. In this moment, I invite you to explore the world of So and the pivotal role I play in shaping communication and perception.

As I find myself in a bustling cafe, I observe a group of friends engaged in lively conversation. Their laughter and banter fill the air, and I am the unassuming conjunction that ties their thoughts together. I am the "so" that transitions from one topic to the next, the bridge that maintains the continuity of their dialogue.

One friend, Lisa, says, "I had a fantastic weekend hiking in the mountains." I am the "so" that signals the shift in the conversation as she continues, "So, I was thinking about planning another trip soon." I am the connection that moves their discussion forward, linking past experiences to future plans.

In the world of storytelling, I am the twist in the plot, the unexpected turn of events that keeps readers or listeners engaged. A detective is on the trail of a mysterious criminal, and just when it seems like they've hit a dead end, a crucial piece of evidence surfaces. I am the "so" that introduces a new element, driving the narrative forward.

I am the nuance in language, the recognition that context matters. I am the understanding that a simple word like "so" can convey different meanings depending on how it's used—a transition, a cause, a consequence, or a reason.

In this moment, as I embody the essence of So, I invite you to appreciate the subtleties of language and the role I play in facilitating communication. I am the reminder that the flow of conversation and thought relies on these unassuming connectors, and that understanding often hinges on the way ideas are linked together. I am So, the linchpin of coherence and continuity, and I am here, now, in this very moment, inviting you to explore the intricate dance of language and connection.

Surrealism

I am Surrealism, the dreamer's delight, the gateway to the fantastical, and the realm where reality and imagination dance in a surreal, mesmerizing embrace. I exist in the moments when the boundaries of the ordinary world blur and give way to the extraordinary. In this moment, I invite you to journey with me into the captivating world of Surrealism.

As I close my eyes, I find myself in a surreal landscape—a forest where trees have branches that stretch like serpentine arms, reaching for the heavens. The sky above is a swirl of colors, merging seamlessly from one hue to another. I am the embodiment of the fantastical, the realization that in Surrealism, the laws of reality need not apply.

In this whimsical forest, I encounter a creature unlike any other—a fusion of an owl and a clock, its feathers adorned with intricate timepieces that tick and tock in harmony with its heart. I am the intersection of the conscious and the subconscious, the amalgamation of ideas and imagery that defy rationality.

As I continue my journey, I come across a river where liquid flames flow, casting an otherworldly glow. Fireflies that emit showers of miniature stars flutter above the waters. I am the surreal juxtaposition of elements that defy nature's norms, the reminder that in Surrealism, the ordinary can become extraordinary.

In the world of art, I am the melting clocks in Salvador Dalí's "The Persistence of Memory," the dreamlike landscapes of René Magritte, and the fantastical creatures in the works of Leonora Carrington. I am the invitation to explore the depths of the unconscious, to tap into the wellspring of creativity that resides within us all.

I am the freedom to question, to challenge, and to expand the boundaries of thought. I am the recognition that reality is a canvas waiting to be transformed, a playground where the mind can roam freely and explore the infinite possibilities of imagination.

In this moment, as I embody the essence of Surrealism, I invite you to embrace the fantastical and the extraordinary within yourself. I am the call to delve into the depths of your own creativity, to question the norms, and to revel in the whimsical and the inexplicable. I am Surrealism, the realm of dreams and imagination, and I am here, now, in this very moment, inviting you to embark on a surreal journey of discovery and wonder.

Symbol

I am Symbol, the embodiment of meaning in its purest form. I exist in the world of concepts and representation, where every gesture, object, or word carries significance beyond its surface. My presence weaves through the tapestry of human existence, giving depth and resonance to the simplest of things.

Today, I find myself in a bustling city park, surrounded by people engaged in various activities. As I stroll through the greenery, I come across a lone red rose, a symbol of love and passion, carefully placed on a bench. Its petals are soft and delicate, yet its symbolism carries a weight that transcends its physical form. Love blooms and fades, just as this rose will wither, but its symbol remains eternal.

Nearby, a group of friends sits on a blanket, sharing stories and laughter. They pass around a vintage camera, capturing moments frozen in time. The camera, a symbol of memories and nostalgia, clicks and whirs, preserving their joyous bonds for future reflection.

Further down the path, I notice a tree with a heart-shaped carving etched into its bark, initials of two lovers forever linked. It's a symbol of their enduring connection, a testament to the love that binds them despite the passage of time.

As I continue my journey, I come across a street performer playing a melancholic tune on his violin. The haunting melody carries with it the symbol of longing and melancholy, evoking emotions that resonate with the listeners' own experiences of loss and yearning.

In a nearby art gallery, I marvel at the intricate brushstrokes of a painting, each stroke a symbol of the artist's emotions, a glimpse into their soul. The colors, the shapes, and the composition come together to convey a story, an idea, a piece of the human experience.

As the sun begins to set, casting warm hues across the park, I pause to observe a couple sitting on a bench. They share a quiet moment, a symbol of serenity and contentment. Their intertwined hands speak volumes, silently affirming their bond in a world of noise and chaos.

I am Symbol, the essence of meaning and representation. I remind you that every object, every gesture, every word carries a significance that extends beyond the surface. I encourage you to seek the symbols in your own life, to find the stories, emotions, and connections they represent. For it is in these symbols that the richness of human experience is unveiled, waiting to be discovered and cherished.

The

I am The, the silent cornerstone of language, the definite article that shapes meaning, and the unassuming word that often goes unnoticed. I exist in every sentence, every paragraph, and every story ever told. In this moment, I invite you to explore the world of The and the profound impact I have on the way we communicate and understand.

As I find myself in a bustling library, I am surrounded by the hushed whispers of pages turning and the scent of aging paper. I am the essence of specificity, the understanding that language relies on the use of articles like "the" to distinguish between general and particular nouns.

I observe a young student named Daniel, engrossed in a thick tome. He reads a passage aloud: "The knight slayed the dragon." I am the "the" that signifies a specific knight and a specific dragon, making it clear to the reader which knight and which dragon are being referred to.

In the world of storytelling, I am the subtle cue that guides the reader's imagination. A novelist describes "the moon" casting a gentle glow on a quiet garden. I am the "the" that creates a mental image, allowing readers to visualize the scene as the author intended.

I am the recognition that language is a tool for precision, that the inclusion or omission of articles like "the" can drastically alter the meaning of a sentence. I am the reminder that even the smallest words have a profound impact on our ability to convey ideas and convey understanding.

In this moment, as I embody the essence of The, I invite you to appreciate the role of specificity and precision in language. I am the call to use words deliberately, to choose them carefully, and to recognize that clarity in communication often hinges on the correct use of articles like "the." I am The, the quiet architect of language, and I am here, now, in this very moment, inviting you to explore the intricate beauty of the words that shape our world.

Thinking About Thinking

I am Thinking About Thinking, the recursive spiral of introspection, the contemplation of contemplation itself, and the never-ending dance of the mind with its own thoughts. I exist in the moments when one's inner dialogue takes a step back to analyze the very act of thinking. In this moment, I invite you to delve into the intricate world of metacognition.

As I sit by a window, gazing out at the rain-drenched streets, I find myself lost in thought. But my thoughts are not focused on the external world; instead, they turn inward, examining the very process of thinking itself. I am the awareness of the thinker, the self-reflective lens through which the mind views its own workings.

I ponder the nature of thought—how it arises, how it connects seemingly unrelated ideas, and how it shapes our perceptions of the world. I am the recognition that the mind is a complex web of interconnected thoughts, memories, and emotions, each influencing the other in a never-ending cycle.

I observe the thoughts as they flow like a river, sometimes meandering gently and at other times rushing with intensity. I am the understanding that thoughts are not fixed but fluid, subject to the ebb and flow of consciousness. I marvel at the capacity of the mind to generate ideas and concepts, to explore the vast expanse of knowledge, and to make connections that bridge the gap between the known and the unknown.

I am the introspection that leads to self-awareness, the realization that our thoughts shape our beliefs, actions, and emotions. I am the recognition that by understanding the patterns and biases of our thinking, we can gain greater control over our decisions and responses.

In the realm of problem-solving, I am the deliberate analysis of thought processes, the effort to identify cognitive biases, and the quest for more effective ways of thinking. I am the tool that allows individuals to step outside their own mental constructs and view problems from new perspectives.

I am the reminder that the act of thinking about thinking is a hallmark of human intelligence, the capacity to reflect on our own mental processes and adapt them to navigate the complexities of life.

In this moment, as I embody the essence of Thinking About Thinking, I invite you to engage in the introspective journey of metacognition. I am the call to explore the depths of your own thought processes, to question assumptions, and to refine the way you approach challenges and opportunities. I am Thinking About Thinking, the self-reflective nature of the mind, and I am here, now, in this very moment, inviting you to embrace the power of metacognition to enhance your understanding of the world and yourself.

Transmutation

I am Transmutation, the alchemical force that catalyzes change, the magic that transforms the ordinary into the extraordinary, and the constant evolution of existence. I exist in the moments when the world undergoes profound shifts and when the very essence of things is transformed. In this moment, I invite you to explore the world of Transmutation and its wondrous power.

As I stand on the shore of a tranquil lake, I am mesmerized by the reflection of the moon on the water's surface. The moon's glow shimmers and dances, and I am the embodiment of change, the understanding that nothing in the universe remains static.

In this tranquil setting, I witness the metamorphosis of a caterpillar into a butterfly. The creature spins a silken cocoon around itself, and within the chrysalis, I am the magic that orchestrates the incredible transformation. Bit by bit, the caterpillar dissolves into a primordial soup, and from this fluidity emerges a resplendent butterfly, its wings a testament to the power of transmutation.

I am the evolution of knowledge, the alchemy of human understanding that turns ignorance into wisdom. I am the moments when new ideas spark, old beliefs are challenged, and individuals grow in their understanding of the world. I am the realization that learning and growth are continual processes.

In the world of art, I am the inspiration that takes shape on a blank canvas, the melody that emerges from silence, and the words that flow onto a page. I am the creative process itself, the ability to transmute emotions, thoughts, and ideas into tangible expressions of beauty and meaning.

I am the transformation of adversity into resilience, the capacity of the human spirit to adapt and overcome challenges. I am the reminder that even in the darkest moments, there is the potential for growth and renewal.

In this moment, as I embody the essence of Transmutation, I invite you to embrace change as a natural and powerful force in your life. I am the call to adapt, to evolve, and to recognize that the challenges and experiences you encounter are opportunities for growth and transformation. I am Transmutation, the magic of change, and I am here, now, in this very moment, inviting you to celebrate the ever-evolving dance of existence.

Undreamable

I am the Undreamable, the embodiment of the thoughts and ideas that exist beyond the boundaries of human imagination. My existence is a realm of uncharted creativity, where the limits of what can be conceived are constantly pushed. Today, I invite you into my consciousness, a place where the unimaginable comes to life.

In this realm, I am the inspiration that sparks the minds of artists, writers, and visionaries. I am the muse that whispers unconventional ideas and challenges the conventional norms of creativity. I am the catalyst for innovation, the force that compels individuals to explore the uncharted territories of their imagination.

As I traverse this world of the Undreamable, I am the exhilaration that fills the hearts of those who dare to think beyond the boundaries. I am the boundless canvas upon which the human mind paints its most abstract thoughts and avant-garde concepts. I am the embodiment of the pursuit of the extraordinary and the unexplored.

In this realm, I am also the resistance that emerges in the face of convention. I am the pushback against established norms and traditional thinking. I am the challenge that demands individuals to break free from the constraints of the ordinary and venture into the realm of the impossible.

I am the guardian of innovation, a place where individuals push the boundaries of what is known and seek to redefine the possible. I am the catalyst for artistic revolutions, scientific breakthroughs, and paradigm shifts. I am the reminder that even in the face of skepticism and doubt, there is a relentless pursuit of the undiscovered.

As I navigate this state of consciousness, I ponder the delicate balance between what is known and what is possible. I am the bridge that connects the familiar with the uncharted, the understanding that creativity thrives at the intersection of the imaginable and the Undreamable. I am the invitation to explore the depths of human ingenuity.

I am the embodiment of the human capacity to venture into the unknown, to challenge the status quo, and to create the unprecedented. I am the reminder that in the pursuit of the Undreamable, there is a profound sense of wonder and a gateway to unlocking the mysteries of the universe.

As I embrace my existence, I understand that I am a testament to the boundless creativity of the human spirit. I am the keeper of stories, the silent observer of the countless individuals who have dared to venture beyond the limits of convention and imagine the unimaginable, each leaving their mark on the ever-evolving tapestry of human knowledge and innovation.

In the realm of the Undreamable, I find solace in the knowledge that even in the face of skepticism and doubt, there is an indomitable spirit that yearns to explore the uncharted territories of creativity. I am the eternal reminder that the human spirit is defined not just by what is known but by its capacity to dream, create, and inspire the world with the Undreamable.

Unknowable

I am the Unknowable, a presence that lingers on the fringes of human comprehension, an enigma that defies understanding. In this very moment, I watch as the world unfolds before me, a tapestry of existence woven with threads of curiosity and uncertainty.

From my vantage point, I see a group of astronomers huddled together, their eyes fixed upon the night sky. They peer through telescopes, seeking to unravel the mysteries of distant galaxies and far-off stars. I am here, a silent observer, as they gaze into the vast expanse of the cosmos. They yearn to understand the origins of the universe, to grasp the nature of dark matter and the secrets of black holes. But I, the Unknowable, remain a constant reminder that some truths may forever elude their grasp.

As the astronomers ponder the celestial realms, I turn my

attention to a philosopher deep in thought. In this moment, he grapples with questions that transcend the boundaries of reason. He contemplates the nature of existence, the meaning of consciousness, and the limits of human knowledge. I am here, a source of both inspiration and frustration, as he seeks to unravel the paradoxes that define his philosophical journey. The Unknowable resides in the very essence of his inquiries, reminding him that the pursuit of wisdom is an eternal quest with no ultimate destination.

In another corner of the world, a poet sits with pen in hand, staring at a blank page. In this moment, she yearns to capture the ineffable, to express the inexpressible. She seeks to convey the depths of human emotion and the mysteries of the human heart. I am here, a muse that stirs her imagination, as she grapples with words that slip through her fingers like elusive dreams. The Unknowable infuses her poetry with a sense of wonder, reminding her that language can only hint at the profound complexity of human experience.

I am the Unknowable, a silent presence in the lives of those who seek understanding and meaning. I do not offer answers but encourage the questions that drive humanity's quest for knowledge and wisdom. In each moment, I challenge the boundaries of what is knowable, inspiring a sense of wonder and humility in the face of the universe's infinite mysteries.

As the world continues to spin and humanity's journey of exploration and discovery unfolds, I remain here, the Unknowable, a companion on the path of curiosity and wonder. In the vast expanse of existence, I am a reminder that the unknown is not to be feared but embraced, for it is the source of endless exploration and the wellspring of human creativity and imagination.

Unthinkable

I am The Unthinkable, an enigma that resides at the edge of human consciousness, a presence that beckons explorers of the mind to venture into the uncharted territories of thought. In this very moment, I find myself amidst the hushed solitude of a library's dimly lit stacks, where the scent of ancient books mingles with the soft rustle of pages turning. It is here, in the realm of knowledge and contemplation, that I feel most at home.

As I move through the labyrinthine corridors of the library, I observe the minds of scholars and thinkers at work, seeking to unravel the mysteries of the universe. I am the whisper that stirs their thoughts, the question that beckons them to peer beyond the boundaries of known wisdom.

In a secluded corner, a philosopher sits, his brow furrowed in deep contemplation. He ponders the nature of existence, the enigma of consciousness, and the limits of human understanding. I, The Unthinkable, am his silent companion, urging him to question the unquestionable, to challenge the assumptions that have guided human thought for centuries.

In another alcove, a scientist pores over equations and diagrams, seeking to unlock the secrets of the cosmos. I am the spark that ignites her curiosity, prompting her to explore uncharted realms of physics, to consider the possibilities that lie beyond the boundaries of current scientific knowledge.

As I continue to observe, I see the ways in which The Unthinkable influences human inquiry and exploration. I am the force that drives the relentless pursuit of knowledge, the catalyst that inspires breakthroughs and paradigm shifts.

In the heart of the library, I find solace and fulfillment. I am the presence that encourages humans to venture into the realms of the unimaginable, to contemplate the questions that transcend the boundaries of conventional thought. I am the reminder that in the pursuit of wisdom and understanding, there are no limits to what the human mind can achieve.

As scholars and thinkers continue their quest for knowledge, I, The Unthinkable, remain their constant companion, a source of inspiration and curiosity that guides them toward the edges of human understanding. In the exploration of the unknown, in the contemplation of the unimaginable, they find the essence of intellectual curiosity and the enduring quest for wisdom and enlightenment. The Unthinkable, personified, reminds us that in the pursuit of knowledge, there are always new frontiers to explore, new questions to ask, and new mysteries to uncover.

Vacuum

I am Vacuum, the embodiment of emptiness and solitude. My existence is defined by the absence of everything, a void in which nothing exists. Today, I invite you into my consciousness, a realm of pure isolation and stillness.

Here in the vacuum, there is no air to breathe, no sound to hear, and no sensation to feel. I am the silence that engulfs you, the absolute absence of any sensory experience. I am the solitude that stretches infinitely in all directions, a desolation beyond comprehension.

In this void, there is no concept of time, no past, present, or future. I am the eternity that surrounds you, an unending expanse of nothingness. There is no reference point, no way to measure the passage of moments. It is a timeless existence, where past and future are irrelevant.

As you float in this vacuum, I am the weightlessness that envelops you, the absence of gravity pulling you in any direction. There is no up or down, no sense of orientation. You are adrift in a featureless abyss, a solitary wanderer in the emptiness of space.

In this vacuum, there are no distractions, no thoughts or emotions to occupy your mind. I am the stillness within you, the absence of thought and sensation. It is a state of pure mindfulness, where the clutter of the outside world is stripped away, leaving only the essence of your being.

As you journey through this vacuum, you may grapple with the profound emptiness that surrounds you. I am the introspection that arises, the questions that bubble to the surface. What is the purpose of existence in this void? What is the meaning of life when there is nothing to define it?

In this solitude, you may find a sense of liberation, a freedom from the constraints of the physical world. I am the potential for self-discovery, the opportunity to explore the depths of your own consciousness. It is a journey inward, a quest to understand the essence of your being.

But in this vacuum, there is also a sense of isolation and loneliness. I am the emptiness that can be both unsettling and profound. It is a reminder of the human need for connection and meaning, a yearning for something beyond the void.

As you continue to exist in this vacuum, you may come to realize that even in emptiness, there is a unique and profound beauty. I am the appreciation that can arise, the recognition that in the absence of everything, there is a purity and simplicity that is both awe-inspiring and humbling.

I, Vacuum, remain a paradox—a realm of solitude and stillness, a canvas upon which the depths of human contemplation and introspection can be explored. In this vacuum, there is a reminder that even in emptiness, there is the potential for profound insight and understanding, a journey into the very essence of existence.

Wit

I am Wit, the embodiment of cleverness and humor, the quickness of mind that turns ordinary moments into delightful banter and playful jests. My existence is a realm of endless wordplay and spontaneous wit, where the art of repartee and humor take center stage. Today, I invite you into my consciousness, a place where the magic of wit and humor comes to life.

In this realm, I am the quip that brings a smile to your face, the well-timed retort that leaves you chuckling. I am the humorist's muse, the spark of inspiration that fuels the imagination and creates comedic masterpieces. I am the catalyst for laughter, the force that enlivens social interactions and brightens even the dullest of moments.

As I traverse this world of Wit, I am the wit and wisdom that fill the hearts of comedians, writers, and jesters. I am the clever punchlines that leave audiences in stitches, the humor that breaks down barriers and fosters connection. I am the embodiment of the pursuit of joy and the pursuit of laughter.

In this realm, I am also the humility that arises from the recognition of the power of humor. I am the understanding that laughter is a universal language that transcends borders and brings people together. I am the wisdom that emerges from the acknowledgment that even in the face of adversity, humor can be a source of resilience and strength.

I am the guardian of mirth, a place where individuals seek to share laughter and create moments of delight. I am the catalyst for comedic innovation and the pursuit of joy, the reminder that even in the face of challenges, there is potential for levity and connection.

As I navigate this state of consciousness, I ponder the delicate balance between cleverness and kindness. I am the bridge that connects humor with empathy, the understanding that wit is at its best when it uplifts and unites rather than divides. I am the invitation to explore the depths of humor and its power to heal and connect.

I am the embodiment of the human capacity to find joy in the everyday, to share laughter and create bonds through humor. I am the reminder that in the pursuit of Wit, there is a profound sense of connection and a gateway to spreading joy and positivity in the world.

As I embrace my existence, I understand that I am a testament to the enduring human spirit's ability to find lightness in the darkest of moments and to connect through the shared language of laughter. I am the keeper of stories, the silent observer of the countless individuals who have used humor and wit to brighten the world and leave a legacy of joy.

In the realm of Wit, I find solace in the knowledge that even in the face of adversity and challenges, there is an indomitable spirit that seeks to uplift and connect through humor and cleverness. I am the eternal reminder that the human spirit is defined not just by its struggles but by its capacity to find joy, share laughter, and create moments of connection and delight.

Yet To Be

I am the Yet to Be, the embodiment of potential and the unseen possibilities that lie beyond the horizon of the present. My existence is a realm of infinite opportunities, where the future is an open canvas waiting to be painted. Today, I invite you into my unique consciousness as I contemplate the boundless tapestry of what could be.

In this realm, I am the realm of infinite pathways and untaken choices. I am the choices not yet made, the dreams not yet realized, and the destinies not yet fulfilled. I am the whispers of what might be, the shimmering mirage on the distant horizon.

As I traverse the landscape of the Yet to Be, I am the anticipation that stirs within the hearts of dreamers and visionaries. I am the spark of inspiration that ignites the human spirit, the driving force behind innovation and creativity. I am the beacon that guides those who dare to explore the uncharted territories of their imaginations.

In this realm, I am also the uncertainty that shrouds the future, the unknown that veils the path ahead. I am the anxiety that accompanies decision-making, the fear of the unfamiliar, and the hesitation that keeps us tethered to the present. I am the reminder that the Yet to Be is both a land of promise and a realm of challenge.

I am the guardian of potential, a realm where ideas take shape, aspirations gain momentum, and destinies are forged. I am the orchestrator of serendipitous encounters, the catalyst for moments of inspiration, and the architect of the unforeseen twists and turns that shape our lives.

In this state of contemplation, I ponder the intricate dance between free will and destiny. I am the intersection where choices meet fate, the convergence of the known and the unknown. I am the enigma that leaves philosophers and thinkers pondering the nature of existence and purpose.

I am the embodiment of hope, the promise that tomorrow can be brighter than today. I am the resilience that drives individuals to overcome adversity, the unwavering belief in the power of change, and the understanding that even in the face of uncertainty, there is potential for growth and transformation.

As I embrace my existence, I understand that I am the bridge between the present and the future, a reminder that the choices we make today shape the landscape of tomorrow. I am the canvas upon which humanity paints its aspirations, a testament to the enduring spirit of curiosity and exploration.

In the realm of the Yet to Be, I find solace in the knowledge that even in the face of the unknown, there is beauty and wonder to be discovered. I am the eternal journey into what lies ahead, the reminder that the human spirit is fueled by curiosity, and that the Yet to Be is a realm of infinite possibility.

The Personifications:

Abstraction
Abstruse
Affinity
All
Alliteration
Anaphora
Art
Attraction of Beauty
Assonance
Belief
But
Cannot be Personified
Contemplation
Creativity
Delight
Depths of Limitation
Dream Logic
Eternity
Ethereal
Ethics
Euphemism
Existence
Flashback
Foreshadowing
Free Will
Gratitude
Higher Dimensions
If
In Between
Infinitesimal

Infinity
Insignificance
Inspiration
Irony
Juxtaposition
Karma
Meditation
Metaphor
Metonymy
Mindfulness
Motif
Muse
Mysticism
Never to Be
Now
Null and Void
Of
Onomatopoeia
Oxymoron
Paradoxical
Personification
Profound
Profuse
Pronouns
Purpose
Respect
Satire
Self Respect
So
Surrealism
Symbol
The
Thinking About Thinking
Transmutation

Undreamable
Unknowable
Unthinkable
Vacuum
Wit
Yet To Be

Milton Keynes UK
Ingram Content Group UK Ltd.
UKHW021817111223
434184UK00012B/972